Mastering Flask

Gain expertise in Flask to create dynamic and powerful web applications

Jack Stouffer

BIRMINGHAM - MUMBAI

Mastering Flask

First published: September 2015

Production reference: 1250915

Published by Packt Publishing Ltd.
Livery Place
35 Livery Street
Birmingham B3 2PB, UK.

ISBN 978-1-78439-365-6

www.packtpub.com

Credits

Author

Jack Stouffer

Reviewers

Nidal Alhariri

Pedro Alejandro Baumann

Ben Chaimberg

Ayun Park

Rotem Yaari

Commissioning Editor

Julian Ursell

Acquisition Editor

Harsha Bharwani

Content Development Editor

Riddhi Tuljapurkar

Technical Editor

Gaurav Suri

Copy Editor

Dipti Mankame

Project Coordinator

Sanchita Mandal

Proofreader

Safis Editing

Indexer

Priya Sane

Production Coordinator

Nitesh Thakur

Cover Work

Nitesh Thakur

About the Author

Jack Stouffer is a programmer who has several years of experience in designing web applications. He switched to Flask two years ago for all his projects. He currently works for Apollo America in Auburn Hills, Michigan and writes internal business tools and software using Python, Flask, and JavaScript. Jack is a believer and supporter of open source technology. When he released his Flask examples with the recommended best practices on GitHub, it became one of the most popular Flask repositories on the site. Jack has also worked as a reviewer for *Flask Framework Cookbook, Packt Publishing*.

Firstly, I would like to thank my two managers at Apollo America, Peter Stouffer and Louise Laing, for giving me a very flexible schedule to write this book, without which I would have never been able to write it in a reasonable amount of time. Secondly, I would like to thank Riddhi Tuljapurkar, who was my content editor and my contact at Packt Publishing for this book, for being flexible when it came to chapter deadlines as well as for giving me good feedback on the chapters. I would also like to thank Llewellyn Rozario for giving me the opportunity to write this book in the first place. Finally, I would like to thank the five technical reviewers, Ayun Park, Ben Chaimberg, Nidal Alhariri, Rotem Yaari, and Pedro Baumann, for investing their time and energy to make the final product a whole lot better than the initial drafts.

About the Reviewers

Nidal Alhariri is an entrepreneur, a full-stack computer programmer, and a technology consultant. He is the creator of Enferno Framework (a Python web framework based on Flask).

He is also the founder and CTO of Level 09 Studios, a web and software development agency based in Dubai and Berlin, which serves clients from different backgrounds, such as international organizations, hotels, luxury real estate, satellite TV, publishing, and many more.

He has been the driving force behind a lot of software applications and web systems for nearly 12 years now and has an excellent record of delivering projects on time and on budget. He has a roster of delighted clients and deep ties to the development community.

Pedro Alejandro Baumann is a cofounder of Athelas Perú, psychotherapist, sysAdmin, and self-taught programmer. He works as a backend developer and sysAdmin for Athelas. He also loves to learn about new technologies, but especially loves to work with Python and dabbles with a few open source projects in his spare time (he mostly adds ZURB foundation to every Flask project that might require it!). He is constantly juggling projects of various kinds. Currently, he is developing a project to inform parents and educators about the reality of video gaming and also writing for a Peruvian coding blog (De Código y Algo más).

I would like to thank my wife, Lucia, who always encouraged me to become a programmer and to make a living out of it. I would also like to thank my co-workers who let me experiment with any technology that I feel like working on at that time.

Ben Chaimberg is a student at the University of Chicago. He was introduced to programming at a young age by his father and hasn't stopped coding since. He is currently working on a full-stack web application in Flask while pursuing his schooling in mathematics.

> I would like to thank my parents for their constant support and commitment, Max for his camaraderie and patience, and Mrs. Kono for her inspiration and concern.

Ayun Park is a 19-year-old software engineer from South Korea. He has been programming in Python since 2011. He can be found at `http://parkayun.kr`.

Rotem Yaari is a software engineer from Israel who's been developing software in Python since 2001. He is actively involved in several open source Python projects, such as the Slash testing framework, the Weber Flask webapp framework, Flask-Loopback, and others.

For the past 8 years, Rotem has been working on backend infrastructure development for data storage start-ups. He specializes in complex software integrations using web services and in high availability infrastructure.

www.PacktPub.com

Support files, eBooks, discount offers, and more

For support files and downloads related to your book, please visit
www.PacktPub.com.

Did you know that Packt offers eBook versions of every book published, with PDF
and ePub files available? You can upgrade to the eBook version at www.PacktPub.
com and as a print book customer, you are entitled to a discount on the eBook copy.
Get in touch with us at service@packtpub.com for more details.

At www.PacktPub.com, you can also read a collection of free technical articles,
sign up for a range of free newsletters and receive exclusive discounts and offers
on Packt books and eBooks.

https://www2.packtpub.com/books/subscription/packtlib

Do you need instant solutions to your IT questions? PacktLib is Packt's online digital
book library. Here, you can search, access, and read Packt's entire library of books.

Why subscribe?

- Fully searchable across every book published by Packt
- Copy and paste, print, and bookmark content
- On demand and accessible via a web browser

Free access for Packt account holders

If you have an account with Packt at www.PacktPub.com, you can use this to access
PacktLib today and view 9 entirely free books. Simply use your login credentials for
immediate access.

Table of Contents

Preface

Flask is a web framework for Python that is specifically designed to provide the minimum amount of functionality that is needed to create web apps. Unlike other web frameworks, especially those in other languages, Flask does not have an entire ecosystem of libraries bundled with it for things such as database querying or form handling. Flask instead prefers to be an implementation agnostic.

The main feature of this setup is that it allows the programmer to design their app and their tools in any way they want. Not providing their own version of common abstractions also means that the standard library can be used much more often than other frameworks, which guarantees their stability and readability by other Python programmers. Because the Flask community is rather large, there are also many different community-provided ways of adding common functionality. One of the main focuses of this book is to introduce these extensions and find out how they can help avoid reinventing the wheel. The best part about these extensions is that if you don't need their extra functionality, you don't need to include them and your app will stay small.

The main downside of this setup is that the vast majority of new Flask users do not know how to properly structure large applications and end up creating an unintelligible and unmaintainable mess of code. This is why the other main focus of this book is how to create a Model View Controller (MVC) architecture with Flask apps.

Originally invented to design desktop user interfaces, the MVC setup allows the data handling (models), user interaction (controllers), and user interface (views) to be separated into three different components.

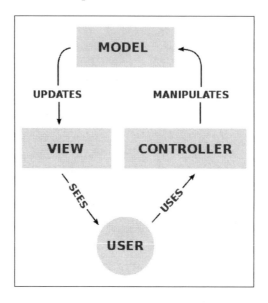

Separating these three different components allows the programmer to reuse code rather than re-implement the same functionality for each web page. For example, if the data handling code wasn't split into its own separate functions, we would have to write the same database connection code and SQL queries in each of the functions that render a web page.

A large amount of research and a lot of painful first-hand experience of what can go wrong while developing web applications has made this book the most comprehensive resource on Flask available, so I sincerely hope that you will enjoy reading it.

What this book covers

Chapter 1, Getting Started, helps readers set up a Flask environment for development using the best practices for Python projects. Readers are given a very basic skeleton Flask app that is built throughout the book.

Chapter 2, Creating Models with SQLAlchemy, shows how to use the Python database library SQLAlchemy in conjunction with Flask to create an object-oriented API for your database.

Chapter 3, Creating Views with Templates, shows how to use Flask's templating system, Jinja, to dynamically create HTML by leveraging your SQLAlchemy models.

Chapter 4, Creating Controllers with Blueprints, covers how to use Flask's blueprints feature in order to organize your view code while also avoiding repeating yourself.

Chapter 5, Advanced Application Structure, using the knowledge gained in the last four chapters, explains how to reorganize the code files in order to create a more maintainable and testable application structure.

Chapter 6, Securing Your App, explains how to use various Flask extensions in order to add a login system with permissions-based access to each view.

Chapter 7, Using NoSQL with Flask, shows what a NoSQL database is and how to integrate one into your application when it allows more powerful features.

Chapter 8, Building RESTful APIs, shows how to provide the data stored in the application's database to third parties in a secure and easy-to-use manner.

Chapter 9, Creating Asynchronous Tasks with Celery, explains how to move expensive or time-consuming programs to the background so the application does not slow down.

Chapter 10, Useful Flask Extensions, explains how to leverage popular Flask extensions in order to make your app faster, add more features, and make debugging easier.

Chapter 11, Building Your Own Extension, teaches you how Flask extensions work and how to create your own.

Chapter 12, Testing Flask Apps, explains how to add unit tests and user interface tests to your app for quality assurance and reducing the amount of buggy code.

Chapter 13, Deploying Flask Apps, explains how to take your completed app from development to being hosted on a live server.

What you need for this book

To get started with this book, all you will need is a text editor of your choice, a web browser, and Python installed on your machine.

Windows, Mac OS X, and Linux users should all be able to easily follow along with the content of this book.

Who this book is for

This book is written for web developers who are already somewhat familiar with Flask and want to take their Flask understanding from introductory to master level.

Conventions

In this book, you will find a number of text styles that distinguish between different kinds of information. Here are some examples of these styles and an explanation of their meaning.

Code words in text, database table names, folder names, filenames, file extensions, pathnames, dummy URLs, user input, and Twitter handles are shown as follows: "The `first()` and `all()` methods return a value and therefore end the chain."

A block of code is set as follows:

```
class User(db.Model):
    id = db.Column(db.Integer(), primary_key=True)
    username = db.Column(db.String(255))
    password = db.Column(db.String(255))
    posts = db.relationship(
        'Post',
        backref='user',
        lazy='dynamic'
    )
```

When we wish to draw your attention to a particular part of a code block, the relevant lines or items are set in bold:

```
from flask.ext.sqlalchemy import SQLAlchemy

app = Flask(__name__)
app.config.from_object(DevConfig)
db = SQLAlchemy(app)
```

Any command-line input or output is written as follows:

```
$ python manage.py db init
```

New terms and important words are shown in bold. Words that you see on the screen, for example, in menus or dialog boxes, appear in the text like this: "Hit another button that says **Download Bootstrap** and you will start to download a Zip file."

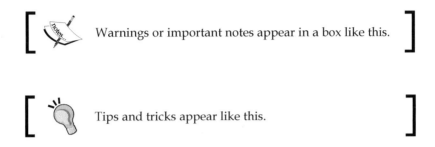

Warnings or important notes appear in a box like this.

Tips and tricks appear like this.

Reader feedback

Feedback from our readers is always welcome. Let us know what you think about this book—what you liked or disliked. Reader feedback is important for us as it helps us develop titles that you will really get the most out of.

To send us general feedback, simply e-mail feedback@packtpub.com, and mention the book's title in the subject of your message.

If there is a topic that you have expertise in and you are interested in either writing or contributing to a book, see our author guide at www.packtpub.com/authors.

Customer support

Now that you are the proud owner of a Packt book, we have a number of things to help you to get the most from your purchase.

Downloading the example code

You can download the example code files from your account at http://www.packtpub.com for all the Packt Publishing books you have purchased. If you purchased this book elsewhere, you can visit http://www.packtpub.com/support and register to have the files e-mailed directly to you.

Errata

Although we have taken every care to ensure the accuracy of our content, mistakes do happen. If you find a mistake in one of our books — maybe a mistake in the text or the code — we would be grateful if you could report this to us. By doing so, you can save other readers from frustration and help us improve subsequent versions of this book. If you find any errata, please report them by visiting http://www.packtpub.com/submit-errata, selecting your book, clicking on the **Errata Submission Form** link, and entering the details of your errata. Once your errata are verified, your submission will be accepted and the errata will be uploaded to our website or added to any list of existing errata under the Errata section of that title.

To view the previously submitted errata, go to https://www.packtpub.com/books/content/support and enter the name of the book in the search field. The required information will appear under the **Errata** section.

Piracy

Piracy of copyrighted material on the Internet is an ongoing problem across all media. At Packt, we take the protection of our copyright and licenses very seriously. If you come across any illegal copies of our works in any form on the Internet, please provide us with the location address or website name immediately so that we can pursue a remedy.

Please contact us at copyright@packtpub.com with a link to the suspected pirated material.

We appreciate your help in protecting our authors and our ability to bring you valuable content.

Questions

If you have a problem with any aspect of this book, you can contact us at questions@packtpub.com, and we will do our best to address the problem.

1
Getting Started

Python is a flexible language that gives programmers the freedom to structure their programming environment. However, a dangerous consequence of this freedom is the ability to not set up a new Python project right from the beginning in order to avoid problems down the road.

For example, you could be halfway through your project and realize that you deleted a file or piece of code five days ago that you need to use now. Consider another example where two of the packages that you wish to use require different versions of the same underlying package. Other than the tools introduced in this chapter, there will be a lot of extra work fixing problems that already have solutions. A little extra work in the beginning can save days of work in the future.

To this end, we will need to install three programs: **Git**, **pip**, and **virtualenv**.

Version control with Git

To protect our project against human error, we will use a version control system called Git. **Version control** is a tool that records changes in files over time. This allows a programmer to see how the code has changed from previous revisions and even revert the code to the previous state. Version control systems also make collaboration easier than ever, as changes can be shared between many different programmers and merged into the current version of the project automatically, without copying and pasting hundreds of lines of code.

Simply put, version control is like backups for your code, only more powerful.

Installing Git

Installing Git is very simple. Simply go to `http://www.git-scm.com/downloads` and click on the **Operating System (OS)** that is being run. A program will begin to download that will walk you through the basic installation process.

Git on Windows

Git was originally developed solely for Unix OSes (for example, Linux, Mac OS X). Consequently, using Git on Windows is not seamless. During the installation, the installer will ask whether you want to install Git alongside the normal Windows Command Prompt. Do not pick this option. Choose the default option that will install a new type of command line on your system named **Bash**, which is the same command line the Unix systems use. Bash is much more powerful than the default Windows command line, and this will be used in all the examples in this book.

 A good introduction to Bash for beginners is located at `http://linuxcommand.org/learning_the_shell.php#contents`.

Git basics

Git is a very complex tool; only the basics that are needed for this book will be covered here.

 To learn more, refer to the Git documentation at `http://www.git-scm.com/doc`.

Git does not track your changes automatically. In order for Git to run properly, we have to give it the following information:

- Which folders to track
- When to save the state of the code
- What to track and what not to

Before we can do anything, we tell Git to create a `git` instance in our directory. In your project directory, run the following in your terminal:

```
$ git init
```

Git will now start to track changes in our project. As `git` tracks our files, we can see the status of our tracked files, and any files that are not tracked, by typing the following command:

```
$ git status
```

Now we can save our first **commit**, which is a snapshot of your code at the time that you run the `commit` command.

```
# In Bash, comments are marked with a #, just like Python
# Add any files that have changes and you wish to save in this commit
$ git add main.py
# Commit the changes, add in your commit message with -m
$ git commit -m"Our first commit"
```

At any point in the future, we can return to this point in our project. Adding files to be committed is called **staging** files in Git. Remember to add stage files only if you are ready to commit them. Once the files are staged, any further changes will not be staged as well. For an example of more advanced Git usage, add any text to your `main.py` file with your text editor and then run the following:

```
# To see the changes from the last commit
$ git diff
# To see the history of your changes
$ git log
# As an example, we will stage main.py
# and then remove any added files from the stage
$ git add main.py
$ git status
$ git reset HEAD main.py
# After any complicated changes, be sure to run status
# to make sure everything went well
$ git status
# lets delete the changes to main.py, reverting to its state at the last commit
# This can only be run on files that aren't staged
$ git checkout -- main.py
```

Your terminal should look something like this:

```
bash-3.2$ git diff
diff --git i/main.py w/main.py
index fc7d1c7..556ab4c 100644
--- i/main.py
+++ w/main.py
@@ -6,7 +6,7 @@ app.config.from_object(DevConfig)

 @app.route('/')
 def home():
-    return 'Hello World!'
+    return '<h1>Hello World!</h1>'

 if __name__ == '__main__':
     app.run()
bash-3.2$ git log
Thu Feb 19 21:11:42 2015 -0500 3d3500b (HEAD, master) Our first commit   [Jack Stouffer]
bash-3.2$ git add main.py
bash-3.2$ git status
On branch master
Changes to be committed:
        modified:   main.py
        new file:   manage.py

Untracked files:
        config.py
        config.pyc
        env/

bash-3.2$
```

The Git system's `checkout` command is rather advanced for this simple introduction, but it is used to change the current status of the Git system's `HEAD` pointer—that is, the current location of our code in the history of our project. This will be shown in the next example.

Now, to see the code in a previous commit, first run this:

```
$ git log
Fri Jan 23 19:16:43 2015 -0500 f01d1e2 Our first commit   [Jack Stouffer]
```

The string of characters next to our commit message, `f01d1e2`, is called the **hash** of our commit. It is the unique identifier of that commit that we can use to return to the saved state. Now, to take the project back to that state, run this:

```
$ git checkout f01d1e2
```

Your Git project is now in a special state where any changes or commits will neither be saved nor affect any commits that were made after the one you checked out. This state is just for viewing old code. To return to the normal mode of Git, run this:

```
$ git checkout master
```

Python package management with pip

In Python, programmers can download libraries from other programmers that extend the functionality of the standard Python library. As you already know from using Flask, a lot of Python's power comes from its large amount of community-created libraries.

However, installing third-party libraries can be a huge pain to do correctly. Say there is a package X that you wish to install. Simple enough, download the Zip file and run `setup.py`, right? Not quite. Package X relies on package Y, which in turn relies on Z and Q. None of this information was listed on package X's website, but they are required to be installed for X to work at all. You then have to find all of the packages one by one and install them, in the hope that the packages you are installing don't require any extra packages themselves.

In order to automate this process, we use **pip**, the Python package manager.

Installing the pip Python package manager on Windows

If you are on Windows, and your installed Python the current version, you already have pip! If your Python installation is not the most recent, the easiest thing to do is to simply reinstall it. Download the Python Windows installer at `https://www.python.org/downloads/`.

In Windows, the variable that controls which programs are accessible from the command line is **path**. To modify your path to include Python and pip, we have to add `C:\Python27` and `C:\Python27\Tools`. Edit the Windows path by opening the Windows menu, right-clicking on **Computer** and clicking on **Properties**. Under **Advanced system settings**, click **Environment Variables....** Scroll down until you find **Path**, double-click it, and add `;C:\Python27;C:\Python27\Tools` to the end.

To make sure you have modified your path correctly, close and reopen your terminal and type the following into the command line:

```
pip --help
```

Downloading the example code

You can download the example code files from your account at `http://www.packtpub.com` for all the Packt Publishing books you have purchased. If you purchased this book elsewhere, you can visit `http://www.packtpub.com/support` and register to have the files e-mailed directly to you.

`pip` should have printed its usage message as shown in the following screenshot:

```
MINGW32:/c/dashboard                                                    _ □ X

jstouffer@PULSAR /c/dashboard (master)
$ pip --help

Usage:
  pip <command> [options]

Commands:
  install            Install packages.
  uninstall          Uninstall packages.
  freeze             Output installed packages in requirements format.
  list               List installed packages.
  show               Show information about installed packages.
  search             Search PyPI for packages.
  wheel              Build wheels from your requirements.
  zip                DEPRECATED. Zip individual packages.
  unzip              DEPRECATED. Unzip individual packages.
  help               Show help for commands.

General Options:
  -h, --help         Show help.
  --isolated         Run pip in an isolated mode, ignoring
                     environment variables and user configuration.
  -v, --verbose      Give more output. Option is additive, and can be
                     used up to 3 times.
```

Installing the pip Python package manager on Mac OS X and Linux

Some Python installations of Linux do not come with pip, and Mac OS X installations don't come with pip by default. To install it, download the `get-pip.py` file from `https://raw.githubusercontent.com/pypa/pip/master/contrib/get-pip.py`.

Once you have downloaded it, run it with elevated privileges using the following:

```
$ sudo python get-pip.py
```

Then pip will be installed automatically.

pip basics

To install a package with `pip`, follow this simple step:

```
$ pip install [package-name]
```

On Mac and Linux, because you are installing programs outside the user-owned folders, you might have to prepend `sudo` to the install commands. To install Flask, simply run this:

```
$ pip install flask
```

Then, all requirements of Flask will be installed for you.

If you want to remove a package that you are no longer using, run this:

```
$ pip uninstall [package-name]
```

If you wish to explore or find a package but don't know its exact name, you may use the search command:

```
$ pip search [search-term]
```

Now that we have a couple of packages installed, it is common courtesy in the Python community to create a list of packages that are required to run the project, so others can quickly install every thing required. This also has the added benefit that any new member of your project will be able to run your code quickly.

This list can be created with pip by running this:

```
$ pip freeze > requirements.txt
```

What exactly did this command do? `pip freeze` run by itself prints out a list of the installed packages and their versions as follows:

```
Flask==0.10.1
itsdangerous==0.24
Jinja2==2.7.3
MarkupSafe==0.23
Werkzeug==0.10.4
wheel==0.24.0
```

The > operator tells Bash to take everything printed by the last command and write it to this file. If you look into your project directory, you will see the new file named `requirements.txt` that contains the output of `pip freeze`.

To install all the packages from this file, a new project maintainer will have to run this:

```
$ pip install -r requirements.txt
```

This tells `pip` to read all the packages listed in `requirements.txt` and install them.

Dependency sandboxing with virtualenv

So you have installed all the packages you want for your new project. Great! But, what happens when we develop the second project some time later that will use newer versions of the same packages? What happens when a library that you wish to use depends on a library you installed for the first project, but it uses an older version? When newer versions of packages contain breaking changes, upgrading them will require extra development work on an older project that you may not be able to afford.

Thankfully, there is virtualenv, a tool that sandboxes your Python projects. The secret to virtualenv is tricking your computer into looking for and installing packages in the project directory rather than in the main Python directory, which allows you to keep them completely separate.

Now that we have pip, to install virtualenv just run this:

```
$ pip install virtualenv
```

virtualenv basics

Let's initialize virtualenv for our project as follows:

```
$ virtualenv env
```

The extra env tells virtualenv to store all the packages into a folder named env. virtualenv requires you to start it before it will sandbox your project:

```
$ source env/bin/activate
# Your prompt should now look like
(env) $
```

The source command tells Bash to run the script env/bin/activate in the context of the current directory. Let's reinstall Flask in our new sandbox as follows:

```
# you won't need sudo anymore
(env) $ pip install flask
# To return to the global Python
(env) $ deactivate
```

However, it goes against the best practices in Git to track what you don't own, so we should avoid tracking the changes in third-party packages. To ignore specific files in our project, the gitignore file is needed.

```
$ touch .gitignore
```

`touch` is the Bash command to create files, and the dot at the start of a file tells Bash to not list its existence unless specifically told to show hidden files. We will create the simple `gitignore` file for now:

```
env/
*.pyc
```

This tells Git to ignore the entire `env` directory and ignore all the files that end with `.pyc` (a *compiled* Python file). When used in this way, the * character is called a **wildcard**.

The beginning of our project

Finally, we can get to our first Flask project. In order to have a complex project at the end of the book, we will need a simple Flask project to start us off.

In the file named `config.py`, add the following:

```
class Config(object):
    pass

class ProdConfig(Config):
    pass

class DevConfig(Config):
    DEBUG = True
```

Now, in another file named `main.py`, add the following:

```
from flask import Flask
from config import DevConfig

app = Flask(__name__)
app.config.from_object(DevConfig)

@app.route('/')
def home():
    return '<h1>Hello World!</h1>'

if __name__ == '__main__':
    app.run()
```

For anyone who is familiar with the base Flask API, this program is very basic. It will just show `Hello World!` on the browser if we navigate to `http://127.0.0.1:5000/`. One point that may be unfamiliar to Flask users is `config.from_object`, rather than `app.config['DEBUG']`. We use `from_object` because in future, multiple configurations will be used, and manually changing every variable when we need to switch between configurations is tedious.

Remember to commit these changes in Git:

```
# The --all flag will tell git to stage all changes you have made
# including deletions and new files
$ git add --all
$ git commit -m "created the base application"
```

 Reminders will no longer be given on when to commit your changes to Git. It is up to readers to develop the habit of committing whenever you reach a stopping point. It is also assumed that you will be operating inside the virtual environment, so all command line prompts will not be prefixed with (env).

Using Flask Script

In order to make next chapters easier for the reader, we will use the first of many **Flask extensions** (packages that extend the functionality of Flask) named **Flask Script**. Flask Script allows programmers to create commands that act within the **Application Context** of Flask—that is, the state in Flask that allows modification of the `Flask` object. Flask Script comes with some default commands to run the server and a python shell in the Application Context. To install Flask Script with `pip`, run this:

```
$ pip install flask-script
```

We will cover more advanced usage of Flask Script in *Chapter 10, Useful Flask Extensions*; for now, let's start with a simple script named `manage.py`. First import Flask Script's objects and your app as follows:

```
from flask.ext.script import Manager, Server
from main import app
```

Then, pass your app to the `Manager` object, which will initialize Flask Script:

```
manager = Manager(app)
```

Now we add our commands. The server is the same as the normal development server run through `main.py`. The `make_shell_context` function will create a Python shell that can be run within the app context. The returned dictionary will tell Flask Script what to import by default:

```
manager.add_command("server", Server())

@manager.shell
def make_shell_context():
    return dict(app=app)
```

 Running the shell through `manage.py` will become necessary later on when the Flask extensions will only initialize when a Flask app is created. Running the default Python shell will cause these extensions to return errors.

Then, end the file with the Python standard way of running only if the user ran this file:

```
if __name__ == "__main__":
    manager.run()
```

You will now be able to run the development server with:

```
$ python manage.py server
```

Use the shell with:

```
$ python manage.py shell
# Lets check if our app imported correctly
>>> app
<Flask 'main'>
```

Summary

Now that we have set up our development environment, we can move on to implementing advanced application features in Flask. Before we can do anything visual, we need something to display. In the next chapter, you will be introduced to, and then master working with, databases in Flask.

2
Creating Models with SQLAlchemy

As previously stated, **models** are a means of abstracting and giving a common interface to data. In most web applications, data is stored and retrieved from a **Relational Database Management System (RDBMS)**, which is a database that holds data in a tabular format with rows and columns and is able to compare data across tables. Some examples include MySQL, Postgres, Oracle, and MSSQL.

In order to create models on top of our database, we will use a Python package named **SQLAlchemy**. SQLAlchemy is a database API at its lowest level and performs **Object Relational Mapping (ORM)** at its highest level. An ORM is a technique to pass and convert data between two sources with different types of systems and data structures. In this case, it converts data between the large amount of types in databases versus the mix of types and objects in Python. Also, a programming language such as Python allows you to have different objects that hold references to each other, and get and set their attributes. An ORM, such as SQLAlchemy, helps translate that into a traditional database.

In order to tie SQLAlchemy into our application context, we will use Flask SQLAlchemy. Flask SQLAlchemy is a convenience layer on top of SQLAlchemy that provides useful defaults and Flask-specific functions. If you are already familiar with SQLAlchemy, then you are free to use it without Flask SQLAlchemy.

By the end of this chapter, we will have a full database schema of our blogging application as well as models interacting with that schema.

Setting up SQLAlchemy

In order to follow along in this chapter, you will need a running database if you do not already have one. If you have never installed a database or you do not have a preference, SQLite is the best option for beginners.

SQLite is a SQL that is fast, works without a server, and is entirely contained in one file. Also, SQLite is natively supported in python. If you choose to go with SQLite, a SQLite database will be created for you in the *Our first model* section.

Python packages

To install Flask SQLAlchemy with `pip`, run the following:

```
$ pip install flask-sqlalchemy
```

We will also need to install specific packages for the database you chose to use that will act as the connector for SQLAlchemy. SQLite users can skip this step:

```
# MySQL
$ pip install PyMySQL
# Postgres
$ pip install psycopg2
# MSSQL
$ pip install pyodbc
# Oracle
$ pip install cx_Oracle
```

Flask SQLAlchemy

Before we can abstract our data, we need to set up Flask SQLAlchemy. SQLAlchemy creates its database connection through a special database URI. This is a string that looks like a URL that contains all the information that SQLAlchemy needs to connect. It takes the general form of the following:

```
databasetype+driver://user:password@ip:port/db_name
```

For each driver you installed previously, the URI would be:

```
# SQLite
sqlite:///database.db
# MySQL
mysql+pymysql://user:password@ip:port/db_name
# Postgres
postgresql+psycopg2://user:password@ip:port/db_name
# MSSQL
mssql+pyodbc://user:password@dsn_name
# Oracle
oracle+cx_oracle://user:password@ip:port/db_name
```

In our `config.py` file, add the URI to the `DevConfig` file with:

```
class DevConfig(Config):
    debug = True
    SQLALCHEMY_DATABASE_URI = "YOUR URI"
```

Our first model

You may have noted that we did not actually create any tables in our database to abstract off of. This is because SQLAlchemy allows us to create either models from tables or tables from our models. This will be covered after we create the first model.

In our `main.py` file, SQLAlchemy must first be initialized with our app as follows:

```
from flask.ext.sqlalchemy import SQLAlchemy

app = Flask(__name__)
app.config.from_object(DevConfig)
db = SQLAlchemy(app)
```

SQLAlchemy will read our app's configuration and automatically connect to our database. Let's create a `User` model to interact with a user table in the `main.py` file:

```
class User(db.Model):
    id = db.Column(db.Integer(), primary_key=True)
    username = db.Column(db.String(255))
    password = db.Column(db.String(255))
```

```
def __init__(self, username):
    self.username = username

def __repr__(self):
    return "<User '{}'>".format(self.username)
```

What have we accomplished? We now have a model that is based on a user table with three columns. When we inherit from db.Model, the entire connection and communication with the database will be already handled for us.

Each class variable that is the db.Column instance represents a column in the database. There is an optional first argument in a db.Column instance that allows us to specify the name of the column in the database. Without it, SQLAlchemy assumes that the name of the variable is the same as the name of the column. Using this, optional variable would look like:

```
username = db.Column('user_name', db.String(255))
```

The second argument to db.Column tells SQLAlchemy what type the column should be treated as. The main types that we will work with in this book are:

- db.String

- db.Text

- db.Integer

- db.Float

- db.Boolean

- db.Date

- db.DateTime

- db.Time

What each type represents is rather simple. The String and Text types take Python strings and translate them to the varchar and text type columns, respectively. The Integer and Float types take any Python number and translate them into the correct type before inserting them into the database. Boolean takes Python True or False statements and if the database has a boolean type, inserts a Boolean into the database. If there is no boolean type in the database, SQLAlchemy automatically translates between Python Booleans and a 0 or a 1 in the database. The Date, DateTime, and Time types use the Python types of the same name from the datetime native library and translate them into the database. The String, Integer, and Float types take an extra argument that tells SQLAlchemy the length limit on our column.

If you wish to truly understand how SQLAlchemy translates your code into SQL queries, add the following to the `DevConfig` file:

```
SQLALCHMEY_ECHO = True
```

This will print out the created queries to the terminal. You may wish to turn this feature off as you get further along in the book, as dozens of queries could be printed to the terminal every page load.

The argument `primary_key` tells SQLAlchemy that this column has the **primary key index** on it. Each SQLAlchemy model *requires* a primary key to function.

SQLAlchemy will assume that the name of your table is the lowercase version of your model class name. However, what if we want our table to be called something other than *users*? To tell SQLAlchemy what name to use, add the `__tablename__` class variable. This is also how you connect to tables that already exist in your database. Just place the name of the table in the string.

```
class User(db.Model):
    __tablename__ = 'user_table_name'

    id = db.Column(db.Integer(), primary_key=True)
    username = db.Column(db.String(255))
    password = db.Column(db.String(255))
```

We don't have to include the `__init__` or `__repr__` functions. If we don't, then SQLAlchemy will automatically create an `__init__` function that accepts the names and values of your columns as keyword arguments.

Creating the user table

Using SQLAlchemy to do the heavy lifting, we will now create the user table in our database. Update `manage.py` to:

```
from main import app, db, User
...
@manager.shell
def make_shell_context():
    return dict(app=app, db=db, User=User)

Style - "db","User" in first line as Code Highlight
```

From now on, whenever we create a new model, import it and add it to the returned `dict`.

This will allow us to work with our models in the shell. Run the shell now and use `db.create_all()` to create all of the tables:

```
$ python manage.py shell
>>> db.create_all()
```

You should now see in your database a table called `users` with the columns specified. Also, if you are using SQLite, you should now see a file named `database.db` in your file structure.

CRUD

In every storage mechanism for data, there are four basic types of functions: **Create, Read, Update, and Delete (CRUD)**. These allow all the basic ways of manipulating and viewing data needed for our web apps. To use these functions, we will use an object on the database named the **session**. Sessions will be explained later in the chapter, but for now, think of them as a storage location for all of our changes to the database.

Creating models

To create a new row in your database using our models, add the model to the `session` and `commit` objects. Adding an object to the session marks its changes for saving, and committing is when the session is saved to the database as follows:

```
>>> user = User(username='fake_name')
>>> db.session.add(user)
>>> db.session.commit()
```

It is simple to add a new row to our table.

Reading models

After we have added data to our database, data can be queried using `Model.query`. For those who use SQLAlchemy, this is shorthand for `db.session.query(Model)`.

For our first example, use `all()` to get all rows in the database as a list.

```
>>> users = User.query.all()
>>> users
[<User 'fake_name'>]
```

When the number of items in the database increases, this query process becomes slower. In SQLAlchmey, as in SQL, we have the limit function to specify the total number of rows we wish to work with.

```
>>> users = User.query.limit(10).all()
```

By default, SQLAlchemy returns the records ordered by their primary keys. To control this, we have the `order_by` function, which is given as:

```
# asending
>>> users = User.query.order_by(User.username).all()
# desending
>>> users = User.query.order_by(User.username.desc()).all()
```

To return just one model, we use `first()` instead of `all()`:

```
>>> user = User.query.first()
>>> user.username
fake_name
```

To return one model by its primary key, use `query.get()`:

```
>>> user = User.query.get(1)
>>> user.username
fake_name
```

All these functions are chainable, which means that they can be appending on to each other to modify the return result. Those of you who are fluent in JavaScript will find this syntax familiar.

```
>>> users = User.query.order_by(
        User.username.desc()
    ).limit(10).first()
```

The `first()` and `all()` methods return a value and therefore end the chain.

There is also a Flask SQLAlchemy-specific method that is called **pagination**, which can be used rather than `first()` or `all()`. This is a convenience method designed to enable the pagination feature that most websites use while displaying a long list of items. The first parameter defines which page the query should return to and the second parameter is the number of items per page. So, if we passed 1 and 10 as the parameters, the first 10 objects would be returned. If we instead passed 2 and 10, objects 11-20 would be returned, and so on.

The pagination method is different from the `first()` and `all()` methods because it returns a pagination object rather than a list of models. For example, if we wanted to get the first 10 items of a fictional `Post` object for the first page in our blog:

```
>>> Post.query.paginate(1, 10)
<flask_sqlalchemy.Pagination at 0x105118f50>
```

This object has several useful properties:

```
>>> page = User.query.paginate(1, 10)
# return the models in the page
>>> page.items
[<User 'fake_name'>]
# what page does this object represent
>>> page.page
1
# How many pages are there
>>> page.pages
1
# are there enough models to make the next or previous page
>>> page.has_prev, page.has_next
(False, False)
# return the next or previous page pagination object
# if one does not exist returns the current page
>>> page.prev(), page.next()
(<flask_sqlalchemy.Pagination at 0x10812da50>,
 <flask_sqlalchemy.Pagination at 0x1081985d0>)
```

Filtering queries

Now we get to the actual power of SQL, that is, filtering results by a set of rules. To get a list of models that satisfy a set of equalities, we use the `query.filter_by` filter. The `query.filter_by` filter takes named arguments that represent the values we are looking for in each column in the database. To get a list of all users with a username of `fake_name`:

```
>>> users = User.query.filter_by(username='fake_name').all()
```

This example is filtering on one value, but multiple values can be passed to the `filter_by` filter. Just like our previous functions, `filter_by` is chainable:

```
>>> users = User.query.order_by(User.username.desc())
        .filter_by(username='fake_name')
        .limit(2)
        .all()
```

`query.filter_by` only works if you know the exact values that you are looking for. This is avoided by passing Python comparison statements to the query with `query.filter`:

```
>>> user = User.query.filter(
        User.id > 1
    ).all()
```

This is a simple example, but `query.filter` accepts any Python comparison. With common Python types, such as `integers`, `strings`, and `dates`, the `==` operator can be used for equality comparisons. If you had an `integer`, `float`, or `date` column, an inequality statement could also be passed with the `>`, `<`, `<=`, and `>=` operators.

We can also translate complex SQL queries with SQLAlchemy functions. For example, to use IN, OR, or NOT SQL comparisons:

```
>>> from sqlalchemy.sql.expression import not_, or_
>>> user = User.query.filter(
        User.username.in_(['fake_name']),
        User.password == None
    ).first()
# find all of the users with a password
>>> user = User.query.filter(
        not_(User.password == None)
    ).first()
# all of these methods are able to be combined
>>> user = User.query.filter(
        or_(not_(User.password == None), User.id >= 1)
    ).first()
```

In SQLAlchemy, comparisons to None are translated to comparisons to NULL.

Updating models

To update the values of models that already exist, apply the `update` method to a query object, that is, before you return the models with a method such as `first()` or `all()`:

```
>>> User.query.filter_by(username='fake_name').update({
        'password': 'test'
    })
# The updated models have already been added to the session
>>> db.session.commit()
```

Deleting models

If we wish to remove a model from the database:

```
>>> user = User.query.filter_by(username='fake_name').first()
>>> db.session.delete(user)
>>> db.session.commit()
```

Relationships between models

Relationships between models in SQLAlchemy are links between two or more models that allow models to reference each other automatically. This allows naturally related data, such as *comments to posts*, to be easily retrieved from the database with its related data. This is where the *R* in RDBMS comes from, and it gives this type of database a large amount of power.

Let's create our first relation. Our blogging website is going to need some blog posts. Each blog post is going to be written by one user, so it makes sense to link posts back to the user that wrote them to easily get all posts by a user. This is an example of a **one-to-many** relationship.

One-to-many

Let's add a model to represent blog posts on our website:

```
class Post(db.Model):
    id = db.Column(db.Integer(), primary_key=True)
    title = db.Column(db.String(255))
    text = db.Column(db.Text())
```

```
    publish_date = db.Column(db.DateTime())
    user_id = db.Column(db.Integer(), db.ForeignKey('user.id'))

    def __init__(self, title):
        self.title = title

    def __repr__(self):
        return "<Post '{}'>".format(self.title)
```

Note the column user_id. Those who are familiar with RDBMSes will know that this represents a **Foreign Key Constraint**. Foreign Key Constraint is a rule in the database that forces the value of user_id to exist in the id column in the user table. This is a check in the database to make sure that Post will always refer to an existing user. The parameter to db.ForeignKey is a string representation of the user_id field. If you have decided to call your user table with __table_name__, you must change this string. This string is used rather than a direct reference with User.id because during initialization of SQLAlchemy, the User object might not exist yet.

The user_id column itself is not enough to tell SQLAlchemy that we have a relationship. We must modify our User model as follows:

```
class User(db.Model):
    id = db.Column(db.Integer(), primary_key=True)
    username = db.Column(db.String(255))
    password = db.Column(db.String(255))
    posts = db.relationship(
        'Post',
        backref='user',
        lazy='dynamic'
    )
```

The db.relationship function creates a virtual column in SQLAlchemy that connects with db.ForeignKey in our Post model. The first parameter is the name of the class that we are referencing. We will cover what backref does soon, but what is the lazy parameter? The lazy parameter controls how SQLAlchemy will load our related objects. subquery would load our relations as soon as our Post object is loaded. This cuts down the number of queries, but will slow down when the number of returned items grows larger. In contrast, with the dynamic option, the related objects will be loaded on access and can be filtered down before returning. This is best if the number of returned objects is or will become large.

We may now access the `User.posts` variable that will return a list of all the posts whose `user_id` field equals our `User.id`. Let's try this now in our shell as follows:

```
>>> user = User.query.get(1)
>>> new_post = Post('Post Title')
>>> new_post.user_id = user.id
>>> user.posts
[]
>>> db.session.add(new_post)
>>> db.session.commit()
>>> user.posts
[<Post 'Post Title'>]
```

Note that we were not able to access our post from our relationship without committing our changes to the database.

The parameter `backref` gives us the ability to access and set our `User` class via `Post.user`. This is given by:

```
>>> second_post = Post('Second Title')
>>> second_post.user = user
>>> db.session.add(second_post)
>>> db.session.commit()
>>> user.posts
[<Post 'Post Title'>, <Post 'Second Title'>]
```

Because `user.posts` is a list, we could have also added our `Post` model to the list to save it automatically:

```
>>> second_post = Post('Second Title')
>>> user.posts.append(second_post)
>>> db.session.add(user)
>>> db.session.commit()
>>> user.posts
[<Post 'Post Title'>, <Post 'Second Title'>]
```

With the `backref` option as dynamic, we can treat our relation column as a query as well as a list:

```
>>> user.posts
[<Post 'Post Title'>, <Post 'Second Title'>]
>>> user.posts.order_by(Post.publish_date.desc()).all()
[<Post 'Second Title'>, <Post 'Post Title'>]
```

Before we move on to our next relationship type, let's add another model for user comments with a one-to-many relationship, which will be used in the book later on:

```python
class Post(db.Model):
    id = db.Column(db.Integer(), primary_key=True)
    title = db.Column(db.String(255))
    text = db.Column(db.Text())
    publish_date = db.Column(db.DateTime())
    comments = db.relationship(
        'Comment',
        backref='post',
        lazy='dynamic'
    )
    user_id = db.Column(db.Integer(), db.ForeignKey('user.id'))

    def __init__(self, title):
        self.title = title

    def __repr__(self):
        return "<Post '{}'>".format(self.title)

class Comment(db.Model):
    id = db.Column(db.Integer(), primary_key=True)
    name = db.Column(db.String(255))
    text = db.Column(db.Text())
    date = db.Column(db.DateTime())
    post_id = db.Column(db.Integer(), db.ForeignKey('post.id'))

    def __repr__(self):
        return "<Comment '{}'>".format(self.text[:15])
```

Many-to-many

What if we have two models that can reference each other, but each model needs to reference more than one of each type? For example, our blog posts will need tags in order for our users to easily group similar posts. Each tag can refer to many posts, but each post can have multiple tags. This type of relation is called a **many-to-many** relationship. Consider the following example:

```python
tags = db.Table('post_tags',
    db.Column('post_id', db.Integer, db.ForeignKey('post.id')),
    db.Column('tag_id', db.Integer, db.ForeignKey('tag.id'))
)

class Post(db.Model):
    id = db.Column(db.Integer(), primary_key=True)
    title = db.Column(db.String(255))
    text = db.Column(db.Text())
    publish_date = db.Column(db.DateTime())
    comments = db.relationship(
        'Comment',
        backref='post',
        lazy='dynamic'
    )
    user_id = db.Column(db.Integer(), db.ForeignKey('user.id'))
    tags = db.relationship(
        'Tag',
        secondary=tags,
        backref=db.backref('posts', lazy='dynamic')
    )

    def __init__(self, title):
        self.title = title

    def __repr__(self):
        return "<Post '{}'>".format(self.title)

class Tag(db.Model):
    id = db.Column(db.Integer(), primary_key=True)
    title = db.Column(db.String(255))

    def __init__(self, title):
        self.title = title

    def __repr__(self):
        return "<Tag '{}'>".format(self.title)
```

The db.Table object is a lower level access to the database than the abstraction of db.Model. The db.Model object rests on top of db.Table and provides a representation of specific rows in the table. The db.Table object is used because there is no need to access individual rows of the table.

The tags variable is used to represent the post_tags table, which contains two rows: one that represents the id of a post, and another that represents the id of a tag. To illustrate how this works, if the table had the following data:

```
post_id    tag_id
1          1
1          3
2          3
2          4
2          5
3          1
3          2
```

SQLAlchemy would translate this to:

- A post with an id of 1 has the tags with ids of 1 and 3
- A post with an id of 2 has the tags with ids of 3, 4, and 5
- A post with an id of 3 has the tags with ids of 1 and 2

You may describe this data as easily as tags being related to posts.

Before the db.relationship function sets up our relationship, but this time it has the secondary parameter. The secondary parameter tells SQLAlchemy that this relationship is stored in the tags table. Let's see this in the following code:

```
>>> post_one = Post.query.filter_by(title='Post Title').first()
>>> post_two = Post.query.filter_by(title='Second Title').first()
>>> tag_one = Tag('Python')
>>> tag_two = Tag('SQLAlchemy')
>>> tag_three = Tag('Flask')
>>> post_one.tags = [tag_two]
>>> post_two.tags = [tag_one, tag_two, tag_three]
>>> tag_two.posts
[<Post 'Post Title'>, <Post 'Second Title'>]
>>> db.session.add(post_one)
>>> db.session.add(post_two)
>>> db.session.commit()
```

As given in the one-to-many relationship, the main relationship column is just a list. The main difference being that the `backref` option is now also a list. Because it's a list, we may add posts to tags from the `tag` object as follows:

```
>>> tag_one.posts.append(post_one)
[<Post 'Post Title'>, <Post 'Second Title'>]
>>> post_one.tags
[<Tag 'SQLAlchemy'>, <Tag 'Python'>]
>>> db.session.add(tag_one)
>>> db.session.commit()
```

The convenience of SQLAlchemy sessions

Now that you understand the power of SQLAlchemy, you can also understand what the SQLAlchemy session object is and why web apps should never be made without them. As stated before, the session can be simply described as an object that tracks the changes in our models and commits them to the database when we tell it to. However, there is a bit more to it than this.

First, the session is the handler for **transactions**. Transactions are sets of changes that are flushed to the database on commit. Transactions provide a lot of hidden functionality. For example, transactions automatically determine which objects will be saved first when objects have relations. You might have noted this when we were saving tags in the previous section. When we added tags to the posts, the session automatically knew to save the tags first despite the fact that we did not add it to be committed. If we are working with raw SQL queries and a database connection, we would have to keep track of which rows are related to which other rows to avoid saving a foreign key reference to an object that does not exist.

Transactions also automatically mark data as stale when changes to an object are saved to the database. When we access the object next, a query is made to the database to update the data, but all happens behind the scenes. If we were not using SQLAlchemy, we would also need to manually track which rows need to updated. If we want to be resource efficient, we only need to query and update those rows.

Second, the session makes it impossible for there to be two different references to the same row in the database. This is accomplished by all queries going through the session (`Model.query` is actually `db.session.query(Model)`), and if the row has already been queried in this transaction, then the pointer to that object will be returned and not a new object. If this check did not exist, two objects that represent the same row could be saved to the database with different changes. This creates subtle bugs that might not be caught instantly.

Keep in mind that Flask SQLAlchemy creates a new session for every request and discards any changes that were not committed at the end of the request, so always remember to save your work.

 For an in-depth look at sessions, the creator of SQLAlchemy, Mike Bayer, gave a talk at PyCon Canada 2012. Refer to *The SQLAlchemy Session - In Depth*, here—`https://www.youtube.com/watch?v=PKAdehPHOMo`.

Database migrations with Alembic

The functionality of web apps change all the time, and with new functionality, we need to change the structure of our database. Whether it's adding or dropping new columns, or creation of new tables, our models will change throughout the life cycle of our app. However, problems quickly arise when the database changes often. When moving our changes from development to production, how can you be sure that you carried over every change without manually comparing each model and its corresponding table? Let's say that you wish to go back in your Git history to see if some earlier version of your app had the same bug that you are now encountering in production. How will you change your database back to the correct schema without a lot of extra work?

As programmers, we hate extra work. Thankfully, there is a tool called **Alembic**, which automatically creates and tracks database migrations from the changes in our SQLAlchemy models. **Database migrations** are records of all the changes of our schema. Alembic allows us to upgrade or downgrade our database to a specific saved version. Upgrading or downgrading by several versions will execute all the files between the two selected versions. The best part of Alembic is that its history files are only Python files. When we create our first migration, we can see how simple the Alembic syntax is.

Alembic does not capture every possible change. For example, it does not record changes on the SQL indexes. After every migration, the reader is encouraged to review the migration file and make any necessary corrections.

We won't work directly with Alembic; instead, we will use **Flask-Migrate**, which is an extension created specifically for SQLAlchemy and works with Flask Script. To install it with `pip`:

```
$ pip install Flask-Migrate
```

To get started, we need to add the command to our `manage.py` file as follows:

```python
from flask.ext.script import Manager, Server
from flask.ext.migrate import Migrate, MigrateCommand

from main import app, db, User, Post, Tag

migrate = Migrate(app, db)

manager = Manager(app)
manager.add_command("server", Server())
manager.add_command('db', MigrateCommand)


@manager.shell
def make_shell_context():
    return dict(app=app, db=db, User=User, Post=Post, Tag=Tag)

if __name__ == "__main__":
    manager.run()
```

We initialized the `Migrate` object with our app and our SQLAlchemy instance, and we made the migrate command callable through `manage.py db`. To see a list of possible commands, run this:

```
$ python manage.py db
```

To start tracking our changes, we use the `init` command as follows:

```
$ python manage.py db init
```

This will create a new folder in our directory named `migrations` that will hold all of our history. Now we start with our first migration:

```
$ python manage.py  db migrate -m"initial migration"
```

This command will cause Alembic to scan our SQLAlchemy object and find all the tables and columns that did not exist before this commit. As this is our first commit, the migration file will be rather long. Be sure to specify the migration message with -m, as it's the easiest way to identify what each migration is doing. Each migration file is stored in the migrations/versions/ folder.

To apply the migration to your database and change your schema, run the following:

```
$ python manage.py db upgrade
```

To return to the previous version, find the version number with the history command and pass it to the downgrade command:

```
$ python manage.py db history
<base> -> 7ded34bc4fb (head), initial migration
$ python manage.py db downgrade 7ded34bc4fb
```

Like Git, a hash marks each migration. This is the main functionality of Alembic, but it is only surface level. Try to align your migrations with your Git commits in order to make it easier to downgrade or upgrade when reverting commits.

Summary

Now that we have data control mastered, we can now move on to displaying our data in our application. The next chapter, *Chapter 3*, *Creating Views with Templates*, will dynamically cover creating HTML based on our models and adding models from our web interface.

3
Creating Views with Templates

Now that we have our data in an easily accessible format, displaying the information in a web page becomes much easier. In this chapter, we will use the included templating language for Flask Jinja, to dynamically create HTML from our SQLAlchemy models. We will also examine Jinja's methods to automate the creation of HTML and modify data for presentation inside a template. Then, the chapter will end with automatically creating and validating HTML forms with Jinja.

Jinja's syntax

Jinja is a templating language written in Python. A **templating language** is a simple format that is designed to help automate the creation of documents. In any templating language, variables passed to the template replace predefined locations in the template. In Jinja, variable substitutions are defined by {{ }}. The {{ }} syntax is called a **variable block**. There are also **control blocks** defined by {% %}, which declare language functions, such as **loops** or if statements. For example, when the Post model from the previous chapter is passed to it, we have the following Jinja code:

```
<h1>{{ post.title }}</h1>
```

This produces the following:

```
<h1>First Post</h1>
```

The variables displayed in a Jinja template can be any Python type or object, as long as they can be converted into a string via the Python function `str()`. For example, a dictionary or a list passed to a template can have its attributes displayed via:

```
{{ your_dict['key'] }}
{{ your_list[0] }}
```

Many programmers prefer to use JavaScript to template and dynamically create their HTML documents to take the HTML rendering load off of the server. This will not be covered in this chapter as it is an advanced JavaScript topic. However, many JavaScript templating engines use the {{ }} syntax as well. If you choose to combine Jinja and your JavaScript templates defined in your HTML files, then wrap the JavaScript templates in the `raw` control block to tell Jinja to ignore them:

```
{% raw %}
<script id="template" type="text/x-handlebars-template">
    <h1>{{title}}</h1>
    <div class="body">
        {{body}}
    </div>
</script>
{% endraw %}
```

Filters

It's a common mistake to believe that Jinja and Python's syntax is the same because of their similarity. However, there is a lot of differences. As you will see in this section, normal Python functions do not really exist. Instead, in Jinja, variables can be passed to built-in functions that modify the variables for display purposes. These functions, named filters, are called in the variable block with the pipe character |:

```
{{ variable | filter_name(*args) }}
```

Otherwise, if no arguments are passed to the filter, the parentheses can be omitted as follows:

```
{{ variable | filter_name }}
```

Filters can also be called control blocks to apply them to blocks of text:

```
{% filter filter_name %}
    A bunch of text
{% endfilter %}
```

There are many filters in Jinja; this book will cover only the most useful filters. For the sake of brevity, in each example, the output of each filter will be listed directly beneath the filter itself.

 For a full list of all the default filters in Jinja, visit `http://jinja.` `pocoo.org/docs/dev/templates/#list-of-builtin-filters.`

default

If the passed variable is `None`, then replace it with a default value as follows:

```
{{ post.date | default('2015-01-01') }}
2015-01-01
```

If you wish to replace the variable with the default value and if the variable evaluates to `False`, then pass `True` to the optional second parameter:

```
{{ '' | default('An empty string', True) }}
An empty string
```

escape

If the passed variable is a string of HTML, the &, <, >, ', and " characters will be printed as HTML escape sequences:

```
{{ "<h1>Title</h1>" | escape }}
&#60;h1&#62;Title&#60;/h1&#62;
```

float

This converts the passed value to a floating point number with the Python `float()` function as follows:

```
{{ 75 | float }}
75.0
```

int

This converts the passed value to an integer with the Python `int()` function as follows:

```
{{ 75.7 | int }}
75
```

join

This is a filter that joins elements of a list with a string and works exactly same as the list method of the same name. It is given as:

```
{{ ['Python', 'SQLAlchemy'] | join(',') }}
Python, SQLAlchemy
```

length

This is a filter that fills the same role as the Python len() function. It is given as:

```
Tag Count: {{ post.tags | length }}
Tag Count: 2
```

round

This rounds off a float to the specified precision:

```
{{ 3.14159265358979323846 | round(1) }}
3.1
```

You may also specify how you want the number to be rounded off:

```
{{ 4.7 | round(1, "common") }}
5
{{ 4.2 | round(1, "common") }}
4
{{ 4.7 | round(1, "floor") }}
4
{{ 4.2 | round(1, "ceil") }}
5
```

The common option rounds like a person would: anything at or above 0.5 is rounded up, and anything less than 0.5 is rounded down. The floor option always rounds the number down, and the ceil option always rounds up, regardless of the decimal.

safe

If you try to insert HTML into your page from a variable, for example, when you wish to display a blog post, Jinja will automatically try to add HTML escape sequences to the output. Look at the following example:

```
{{ "<h1>Post Title</h1>" }}
&lt;h1&gt;Post Title&lt;/h1&gt;
```

This is a necessary security feature. When an application has inputs that allow users to submit arbitrary text, it allows a malicious user to input HTML code. For example, if a user were to submit a script tag as a comment and Jinja didn't have this feature, the script would be executed on all the browsers that visited the page.

However, we still need a way to display HTML that we know is safe to show, such as the HTML of our blog posts. We can achieve this using the `safe` filter as follows:

```
{{ "<h1>Post Title</h1>" | safe }}
<h1>Post Title</h1>
```

title

We capitalize a string using title case format as follows:

```
{{ "post title" | title }}
Post Title
```

tojson

We can pass the variable to the Python `json.dumps` function. Remember that your passed object must be serializable by the `json` module.

```
{{ {'key': False, 'key2': None, 'key3': 45} | tojson }}
{key: false, key2: null, key3: 45}
```

This feature is most commonly used to pass SQLAlchemy models to JavaScript MVC frameworks on page load rather than waiting for an AJAX request. If you use `tojson` in this way, remember to pass the result to the `safe` filter as well to make sure that you don't get HTML escape sequences in your JavaScript. Here is an example with a `Backbone.js`, a popular JavaScript MVC framework, collection of models:

```
var collection - new PostCollection({{ posts | tojson | safe }});
```

truncate

This takes a long string and returns a string cutoff at the specified length in characters and appends an ellipses:

```
{{ "A Longer Post Body Than We Want" | truncate(10) }}
A Longer...
```

By default, any words that are cut in the middle are discarded. To disable this, pass `True` as an extra parameter:

```
{{ "A Longer Post Body Than We Want" | truncate(10, True) }}
A Longer P...
```

Custom filters

Adding your own filter into Jinja is as simple as writing a Python function. To understand custom filters, we will look at an example. Our simple filter will count the number of occurrences of a substring in a string and return it. Look at the following call:

```
{{ variable | filter_name("string") }}
```

This will be changed to:

```
filter_name(variable, "string")
```

We can define our filter as:

```
def count_substring(string, sub):
    return string.count(sub)
```

To add this function to the list of available filters, we have to manually add it to the `filters` dictionary of the `jinja_env` object in our `main.py` file:

```
app.jinja_env.filters['count_substring'] = count_substring
```

Comments

Comments in the template are defined by {# #}, will be ignored by Jinja, and will not be in the returned HTML code:

```
{# Note to the maintainers of this code #}
```

if statements

`if` statements in Jinja are similar to Python's `if` statements. Anything that returns, or is, a Boolean determines the flow of the code:

```
{%if user.is_logged_in() %}
    <a href='/logout'>Logout</a>
{% else %}
    <a href='/login'>Login</a>
{% endif %}
```

Filters can also be used in `if` statements:

```
{% if comments | length > 0 %}
    There are {{ comments | length }} comments
{% else %}
    There are no comments
{% endif %}
```

Loops

We can use loops in Jinja to iterate over any list or generator function:

```
{% for post in posts %}
    <div>
        <h1>{{ post.title }}</h1>
        <p>{{ post.text | safe }}</p>
    </div>
{% endfor %}
```

Loops and `if` statements can be combined to mimic the `break` functionality in Python loops. In this example, the loop will only use the post if `post.text` is not `None`:

```
{% for post in posts if post.text %}
    <div>
        <h1>{{ post.title }}</h1>
        <p>{{ post.text | safe }}</p>
    </div>
{% endfor %}
```

Inside the loop, you have access to a special variable named `loop`, which gives you access to information about the `for` loop. For example, if we want to know the current index of the current loop to emulate the `enumerate` function in Python, we may use the index variable of the loop variable as follows:

```
{% for post in posts %}
    {{ loop.index }}. {{ post.title }}
{% endfor %}
```

This will produce the following output:

```
1. Post Title
2. Second Post
```

All the variables and functions that the `loop` object exposes are listed in the following table:

Variable	Description
loop.index	The current iteration of the loop (1 indexed)
loop.index0	The current iteration of the loop (0 indexed)
loop.revindex	The number of iterations from the end of the loop (1 indexed)
loop.revindex0	The number of iterations from the end of the loop (0 indexed)
loop.first	True if the current item is first in the iterator
loop.last	True if the current item is last in the iterator
loop.length	The number of items in the iterator
loop.cycle	The helper function to cycle between the items in the iterator, which is explained later
loop.depth	Indicates how deep in a recursive loop the loop currently is (starts at level 1)
loop.depth0	Indicates how deep in a recursive loop the loop currently is (starts at level 0)

The `cycle` function is a function that goes through an iterator one item at a time at every loop. We may use the previous example to demonstrate:

```
{% for post in posts %}
    {{ loop.cycle('odd', 'even') }} {{ post.title }}
{% endfor %}
```

This will output:

```
odd Post Title
even Second Post
```

Macros

A **macro** is best understood as a function in Jinja that returns a template or HTML string. This is used to avoid code that is repeated over and over again and reduce it to one function call. For example, the following is a macro to add a Bootstrap CSS input and a label to your template:

```
{% macro input(name, label, value='', type='text') %}
    <div class="form-group">
        <label for"{{ name }}">{{ label }}</label>
```

```
        <input type="{{ type }}" name="{{ name }}"
            value="{{ value | escape }}" class="form-control">
    </div>
{% endmacro %}
```

Now to quickly add an input to a form in any template, call your macro using the following:

```
{{ input('name', 'Name') }}
```

This will output:

```
<div class="form-group">
    <label for"name">Name</label>
    <input type="text" name="name" value="" class="form-control">
</div>
```

Flask-specific variables and functions

Flask makes several functions and objects available to you by default in your template.

config

Flask makes the current `config` object available in templates:

```
{{ config.SQLALCHEMY_DATABASE_URI }}
sqlite:///database.db
```

request

This is the Flask `request` object for the current request.

```
{{ request.url }}
http://127.0.0.1/
```

session

The Flask `session` object is:

```
{{ session.new }}
True
```

url_for()

The `url_for` function returns the URL of a route by giving the route function name as a parameter. This allows URLs to be changed without worrying about where links will break.

```
{{ url_for('home') }}
/
```

If we had a route that had positional arguments in the URL, we pass them as `kwargs`. They will be filled in for us in the resulting URL as:

```
{{ url_for('post', post_id=1) }}
/post/1
```

get_flashed_messages()

This returns a list of all the messages passed through the `flash()` function in Flask. The `flash` function is a simple function that queues messages, which are just Python strings, for the `get_flashed_messages` function to consume.

```
{% for message in get_flashed_messages() %}
    {{ message }}
{% endfor %}
```

Creating our views

To get started, we need to create a new folder named `templates`, in our project directory. This folder will store all of our Jinja files, which are just HTML files with Jinja syntax mixed in. Our first template will be our home page, which will be a list of the first 10 posts with summaries. There will also be a view for a post that will just show the post content, comments on the page, links to the author user page, and links to tag pages. There will also be user and tag pages that show all the posts by a user and all the posts with a specific tag. Each page will also have a sidebar showing the five most recent posts and the top five most used tags.

The view function

Because each page will have the same sidebar information, we can break that into a separate function to simplify our code. In the `main.py` file, add the following code:

```
from sqlalchemy import func
...
def sidebar_data():
```

```
recent = Post.query.order_by(
    Post.publish_date.desc()
).limit(5).all()
top_tags = db.session.query(
    Tag, func.count(tags.c.post_id).label('total')
).join(
    tags
).group_by(Tag).order_by('total DESC').limit(5).all()

return recent, top_tags
```

The most recent posts query is straight forward, but the most popular tags query
looks somewhat familiar, yet a little odd. This is a bit beyond the scope of this book,
but using the SQLAlchemy `func` library to return a count, we are able to order our
tags by the most used tags. The `func` function is explained in detail at `http://
docs.sqlalchemy.org/en/rel_1_0/core/sqlelement.html#sqlalchemy.sql.
expression.func.`

The home page function in `main.py` will need all the posts in a pagination object
and the sidebar information:

```
from flask import Flask, render_template
...
@app.route('/')
@app.route('/<int:page>')
def home(page=1):
    posts = Post.query.order_by(
        Post.publish_date.desc()
    ).paginate(page, 10)
    recent, top_tags = sidebar_data()

    return render_template(
        'home.html',
        posts=posts,
        recent=recent,
        top_tags=top_tags
    )
```

Here, we finally see how Flask and Jinja tie together. The Flask function
`render_template` takes the name of a file in the folder templates and passes
all the `kwargs` to the template as variables. Also, our `home` function now has
multiple routes to handle pagination and will default to the first page if there
is nothing after the slash.

Now that you have all the pieces of knowledge that you need to write view functions, I challenge you to try to write the rest of the view functions based on the preceding descriptions. After you have tried, compare your results to the following:

```python
@app.route('/post/<int:post_id>')
def post(post_id):
    post = Post.query.get_or_404(post_id)
    tags = post.tags
    comments = post.comments.order_by(Comment.date.desc()).all()
    recent, top_tags = sidebar_data()

    return render_template(
        'post.html',
        post=post,
        tags=tags,
        comments=comments,
        recent=recent,
        top_tags=top_tags
    )


@app.route('/tag/<string:tag_name>')
def tag(tag_name):
    tag = Tag.query.filter_by(title=tag_name).first_or_404()
    posts = tag.posts.order_by(Post.publish_date.desc()).all()
    recent, top_tags = sidebar_data()

    return render_template(
        'tag.html',
        tag=tag,
        posts=posts,
        recent=recent,
        top_tags=top_tags
    )


@app.route('/user/<string:username>')
def user(username):
    user = User.query.filter_by(username=username).first_or_404()
    posts = user.posts.order_by(Post.publish_date.desc()).all()
    recent, top_tags = sidebar_data()
    return render_template(
        'user.html',
        user=user,
        posts=posts,
        recent=recent,
        top_tags=top_tags
    )
```

After all of your views are written, the only thing left to do is to write the templates.

Writing the templates and inheritance

Because this book does not focus on interface design, we will use the CSS library Bootstrap and avoid writing custom CSS. If you have never used it before, **Bootstrap** is a set of default CSS rules that make your website work well across all browsers and has tools that allow you to easily control the layout of your website. To download Bootstrap, go to `http://getbootstrap.com/` and hit the button that says **Download Bootstrap**. Hit another button that says **Download Bootstrap** and you will start to download a Zip file. Unzip this file into your project directory and rename the folder to `static`. The `static` folder must be at the same directory level as the `main.py` file for Flask to automatically find the files. From now on, this is where we will keep our CSS, font, images, and JavaScript files.

Because every route will have a template assigned to it, each template will need the requisite HTML **boilerplate** code with our meta information, style sheets, common JavaScript libraries, and so on. To keep our templates **DRY (Don't Repeat Yourself)**, we will use one of the most powerful features of Jinja, template inheritance. **Template inheritance** is when a child template can import a base template as a starting point and only replace marked sections in the base. To start our base template, we need a basic HTML skeleton as follows:

```html
<!DOCTYPE html>
<html>
<head>
  <meta charset="utf-8">
  <meta http-equiv="X-UA-Compatible" content="IE=edge">
  <meta name="viewport" content="width=device-width, initial-
    scale=1">
  <title>{% block title %}Blog{% endblock %}</title>
  <link rel="stylesheet" href="{{ url_for('static',
    filename='css/bootstrap.min.css') }}">
</head>
<body>
  <div class="container">
    <div class="jumbotron">
      <h1><a href="{{ url_for('home') }}">My Blog</a></h1>
        <p>Welcome to the blog!</p>
    </div>
    {% block body %}
    {% endblock %}
  </div>
```

```
<script src="{{ url_for('static', filename='js/jquery.min.js')
    }}">></script>
<script src="{{ url_for('static',
    filename='js/bootstrap.min.js') }}">></script>
</body>
</html>
```

Save this as `base.html` in your `templates` directory. The `block` control block is used in inheritance to mark sections to be replaceable by the child template. Because we will use pagination in several different pages, let's create a macro to render a pagination widget:

```
{% macro render_pagination(pagination, endpoint) %}
  <nav>
    <ul class="pagination">
      <li>
        <a href="{{ url_for('home', page=pagination.prev().page)
          }}" aria-label="Previous">
          <span aria-hidden="true">&laquo;</span>
        </a>
      </li>
      {% for page in pagination.iter_pages() %}
        {% if page %}
          {% if page != pagination.page %}
            <li>
              <a href="{{ url_for(endpoint, page=page) }}">
                {{ page }}
              </a>
            </li>
          {% else %}
            <li><a href="">{{ page }}</a></li>
          {% endif %}
        {% else %}
          <li><a>...</a><li>
        {% endif %}
      {% endfor %}
      <li>
        <a href="{{ url_for('home', page=pagination.next().page)
          }}" aria-label="Next">
          <span aria-hidden="true">&raquo;</span>
        </a>
      </li>
    </ul>
  </nav>
{% endmacro %}
```

This macro takes a Flask SQLAlchemy pagination object and a view function name and constructs a Bootstrap list of page links. Add this to the top of `base.html` so that all the pages that inherit from it will have access to it.

The home page template

To inherit a template, the `extends` control block is used:

```
{% extends "base.html" %}
{% block title %}Home{% endblock %}
```

This template will use all the HTML `base.html` but replace the data in the `title` block. If we do not declare a `title` block, the content in `base.html` would remain unchanged. Save this template as `index.html`. Now we can see this in action. Open `http://127.0.0.1:5000/` on your browser and you should see the following:

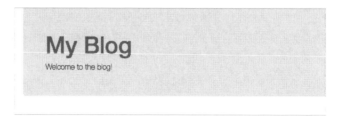

At this point, it is easier to develop and mock UIs if you have representative fake data. Because we only have two posts and manually adding a large amount of models from the command line is tedious (which we shall fix in *Chapter 10, Useful Flash Extensions*), let's use the following script to add 100 example posts:

```python
import random
import datetime

user = User.query.get(1)

tag_one = Tag('Python')
tag_two = Tag('Flask')
tag_three = Tag('SQLAlechemy')
tag_four = Tag('Jinja')
tag_list = [tag_one, tag_two, tag_three, tag_four]

s = "Example text"

for i in xrange(100):
```

```
new_post = Post("Post " + str(i))
new_post.user = user
new_post.publish_date = datetime.datetime.now()
new_post.text = s
new_post.tags = random.sample(tag_list, random.randint(1, 3))
db.session.add(new_post)

db.session.commit()
```

This script is simple for loop that sets all the attributes of a new post and randomizes what tags the post has. Now, to begin developing our templates in earnest, we will start by adding the following to the home page: summaries of our blog posts with links, the most recent blog posts, and the most commonly used tags.

Now, let's add our content to home.html:

```
{% block body %}
<div class="row">
  <div class="col-lg-9">
    {% for post in posts.items %}
    <div class="row">
      <div class="col-lg-12">
        <h1>{{ post.title }}</h1>
      </div>
    </div>
    <div class="row">
      <div class="col-lg-12">
        {{ post.text | truncate(255) | safe }}
        <a href="{{
          url_for('posts', post_id=post.id)
          }}">Read More</a>
      </div>
    </div>
    {% endfor %}
  </div>
  <div class="col-lg-3">
    <div class="row">
      <h5>Recent Posts</h5>
      <ul>
        {% for post in recent %}
        <li><a href="{{
          url_for('post', post_id=post.id)
```

```
      }}">{{ post.title }}</a></li>
    {% endfor %}
  </ul>
</div>
<div class="row">
  <h5>Popular Tags</h5>
  <ul>
    {% for tag in top_tags %}
    <li><a href="{{ url_for('tag', tag_name=tag[0].title)
      }}">{{ tag[0].title }}</a></li>
    {% endfor %}
  </ul>
</div>
  </div>
</div>
{% endblock %}
```

All the other pages will take this general form of content in the middle with a sidebar of links to popular content.

Writing the other templates

Now that you know the ins and outs of inheritance and you know which data is going to go to each template, I will pose the same challenge as the previous section. Try to write the content sections of the remaining templates. After finishing it, you should be able to freely navigate around your blog, click on posts, and view user pages. There is one final bit of functionality to add in this chapter—the ability for readers to add comments.

Flask WTForms

Adding forms in your application seems to be an easy task, but when you start coding the server-side code, the task of validating user input grows bigger and bigger as the form becomes more complex. Security is paramount as the data is from an untrustworthy source and is going to be entered in the database. **WTForms** is a library that handles server form validation for you by checking input against common form types. Flask WTForms is a Flask extension on top of WTForms that add features, such as Jinja HTML rendering, and protects you against attacks, such as **SQL injection** and **cross-site request forgery**. To install Flask WTForms and WTForms, we have:

```
$ pip install Flask-WTF
```

Protecting yourself against SQL injection and cross-site request forgery is extremely important, as these are the most common forms of attacks your website will receive. To learn more about these attacks, visit https://en.wikipedia.org/wiki/SQL_injection and https://en.wikipedia.org/wiki/Cross-site_request_forgery for SQL injection and cross-site request forgery, respectively.

To have Flask WTForms' security measures working properly, we will need a secret key. A **secret key** is a random string of characters that will be used to cryptographically sign anything that needs to be tested for its authenticity. This cannot be any string; it must be randomized to avoid weakening the strength of the security protections. To generate a random string, type the following into Bash:

```
$ cat /dev/urandom | tr -cd 'a-f0-9' | head -c 32
```

If you are using Mac, type the following:

```
cat /dev/urandom | env LC_CTYPE=C tr -cd 'a-f0-9' | head -c 32
```

Add the output in config.py on the Config object:

```
class Config(object):
    SECRET_KEY = 'Your key here'
```

WTForms basics

There are three main parts of WTForms—**forms**, **fields**, and **validators**. Fields are representations of input fields and do rudimentary type checking, and validators are functions attached to fields that make sure that the data submitted in the form is within our constraints. The form is a class that contains fields and validators and validates itself on a POST request. Let's see this in action to get a better idea. In the main.py file, add the following:

```
from flask_wtf import Form
from wtforms import StringField, TextAreaField
from wtforms.validators import DataRequired, Length
...
class CommentForm(Form):
    name = StringField(
        'Name',
        validators=[DataRequired(), Length(max=255)]
    )
    text = TextAreaField(u'Comment', validators=[DataRequired()])
```

Here we have a class that inherits from Flask WTForm's `Form` object and defines inputs with class variables that equal WTForm fields. The fields take an optional parameter `validators`, a list of WTForm validators that will be applied to our data. The most commonly used fields are:

- `fields.DateField`

  This represents a Python `Date` object and takes an optional parameter format that takes a `stftime` format string to translate the data.

- `fields.IntegerField`

  This attempts to coerce passed data to an integer and is rendered in the template as a number input.

- `fields.FloatField`

  This attempts to coerce passed data to a float and is rendered in the template as a number input.

- `fields.RadioField`

  This represents a set of radio inputs and takes a parameter `choices`, that is, a list of tuples that act as the displayed value and the returned value.

- `fields.SelectField`

  Along with `SelectMultipleField`, it represents a set of radio inputs. Takes a parameter `choices`, that is, a list of tuples that act as the displayed and returned values.

- `fields.StringField`

  This represents a normal text input and will attempt to coerce the returned data to a string.

 For a full list of validators and fields, visit the WTForms documentation at `http://wtforms.readthedocs.org`.

The most common validators are as follows:

- `validators.DataRequired()`
- `validators.Email()`
- `validators.Length(min=-1, max=-1)`

- validators.NumberRange(min=None, max=None)
- validators.Optional()
- validators.Regexp(regex)
- validators.URL()

Each of these validations follows the Pythonic naming scheme. Therefore, they are rather straight forward on what they do. All validators take an optional parameter named message, which is the error message that will be returned if the validator fails. If message is not set, it uses same defaults.

Custom validators

Writing a custom validation function is very simple. All that is required is to write a function that takes the form object and the field object as parameters and raises a WTForm.ValidationError if the data does not pass the test. Here is an example of a custom e-mail validator:

```
import re
import wtforms
def custom_email(form, field):
  if not re.match(r"[^@]+@[^@]+\.[^@]+", field.data):
    raise wtforms.ValidationError('Field must be a valid email
      address.')
```

To use this function, just add it to the list of validators for your field.

Posting comments

Now that we have our comment form and we understand how to build it, we need to add it to the start of our post view:

```
@app.route('/post/<int:post_id>', methods=('GET', 'POST'))
def post(post_id):
form = CommentForm()
if form.validate_on_submit():
        new_comment = Comment()
    new_comment.name = form.name.data
    new_comment.text = form.text.data
    new_comment.post_id = post_id
    new_comment.date = datetime.datetime.now()
```

```
db.session.add(new_comment)
db.session.commit()
post = Post.query.get_or_404(post_id)
tags = post.tags
comments = post.comments.order_by(Comment.date.desc()).all()
recent, top_tags = sidebar_data()

return render_template(
    'post.html',
    post=post,
    tags=tags,
    comments=comments,
    recent=recent,
    top_tags=top_tags,
    form=form
)
```

First, we add the POST method to the list of allowed method to our view. Then, a new instance of our form object is created. The validate_on_submit() method then checks whether the Flask request is a POST request. If it is a POST request, it sends the request form data to the form object. If the data is validated, then validate_on_submit() returns True and adds the data to the form object. We then take the data from each field, populate a new comment, and add it to the database. Finally, we add the form to the variable to be sent to the template, so we can add the form to our post.html file:

```html
<div class="col-lg-12">
  <h3>New Comment:</h3>
  <form method="POST" action="{{ url_for('post', post_id=post.id)
    }}">
    {{ form.hidden_tag() }}
    <div class="form-group">
      {{ form.name.label }}
      {% if form.name.errors %}
        {% for e in form.name.errors %}
          <p class="help-block">{{ e }}</p>
        {% endfor %}
      {% endif %}
      {{ form.name(class_='form-control') }}
    </div>
    <div class="form-group">
      {{ form.text.label }}
      {% if form.text.errors %}
```

```
{% for e in form.text.errors %}
    <p class="help-block">{{ e }}</p>
{% endfor %}
{% endif %}
{{ form.text(class_='form-control') }}
</div>
<input class="btn btn-primary" type="submit" value="Add
  Comment">
</form>
</div>
```

There are several new things happing here. First, the `form.hidden_tag()` method adds an anti-cross-site request forgery measure automatically. Second, the `field.errors` list is used to render any messages that our validators send if validation fails. Third, calling the field itself as a method will render the HTML code of that field. Finally, calling `field.label` will automatically create an HTML label for our input. Now, adding information to the fields and pressing the submit button should add your comment!

This would look like the following screenshot:

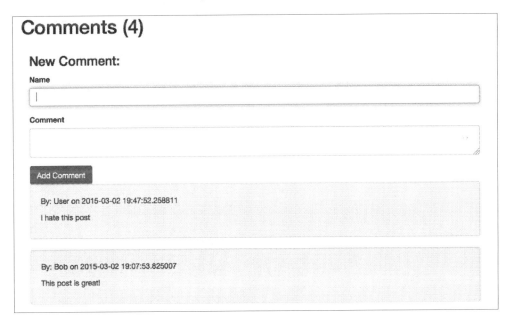

One final challenge for the reader is to make a macro that takes a `form` object and an endpoint to send the `POST` request to and autogenerate HTML for the entire form tag. Refer to the WTForms documents if you get stuck. It's tricky, but not too difficult.

Summary

Now, after only three chapters, you already have a fully functional blog. This is where a lot of books on web development technologies would end. However, there are still 10 more chapters to go to turn your utilitarian blog into something that a user would actually use for their website. In the next chapter, we will focus on structuring Flask apps to accommodate long-term development and larger scale projects.

4
Creating Controllers with Blueprints

The final piece of the **Model View Controller (MVC)** equation is controllers. We have already seen the basic usage of the view functions in our main.py file. Now, the more complex and powerful versions will be introduced, and we will turn our disparate view functions in cohesive wholes. We will also discuss the internals of how Flask handles the lifetime of an HTTP request and advanced ways to define Flask views.

Request setup, teardown, and application globals

In some cases, a request-specific variable is needed across all view functions and needs to be accessed from the template as well. To achieve this, we can use Flask's decorator function @app.before_request and the object g. The function @app.before_request is executed every time before a new request is made. The Flask object g is a thread-safe store of any data that needs to be kept for each specific request. At the end of the request, the object is destroyed, and a new object is spawned at the start of a new request. For example, the following code checks whether the Flask session variable contains an entry for a logged in user; if it exists, it adds the User object to g:

```
from flask import g, session, abort, render_template

@app.before_request
def before_request():
    if 'user_id' in session:
```

```
        g.user = User.query.get(session['user_id'])

@app.route('/restricted')
def admin():
    if g.user is None:
        abort(403)
    return render_template('admin.html')
```

Multiple functions can be decorated with @app.before_request, and they all will be executed before the requested view function is executed. There also exists a decorator @app.teardown_request, called after the end of every request. Keep in mind that this method of handling user logins is meant as an example and is not secure. The recommend method is covered in *Chapter 6, Securing Your App.*

Error pages

Displaying a browser's default error pages to the end user is jarring as the user loses all context of your app, and they must hit the *back* button to return to your site. To display your own templates when an error is returned with the Flask abort() function, use the errorhandler decorator function:

```
@app.errorhandler(404)
def page_not_found(error):
    return render_template('page_not_found.html'), 404
```

The errorhandler is also useful to translate internal server errors and HTTP 500 code into user-friendly error pages. The app.errorhandler() function may take either one or many HTTP status codes to define which code it will act on. The returning of a tuple instead of just an HTML string allows you to define the HTTP status code of the Response object. By default, this is set to 200.

Class-based views

In most Flask apps, views are handled by functions. However, when many views share common functionality or there are pieces of code that could be broken out into separate functions, it would be useful to implement our views as classes to take advantage of inheritance.

For example, if we have views that render a template, we could create a generic view class that keeps our code *DRY*:

```
from flask.views import View

class GenericView(View):
    def __init__(self, template):
        self.template = template
        super(GenericView, self).__init__()

    def dispatch_request(self):
        return render_template(self.template)

app.add_url_rule(
    '/', view_func=GenericView.as_view(
        'home', template='home.html'
    )
)
```

The first thing to note about this code is the `dispatch_request()` function in our view class. This is the function in our view that acts as the normal view function and returns an HTML string. The `app.add_url_rule()` function mimics the `app.route()` function as it ties a route to a function call. The first argument defines the route of the function, and the `view_func` parameter defines the function that handles the route. The `View.as_view()` method is passed to the `view_func` parameter because it transforms the `View` class into a view function. The first argument defines the name of the view function, so functions such as `url_for()` can route to it. The remaining parameters are passed to the `__init__` function of the `View` class.

Like the normal view functions, HTTP methods other than GET must be explicitly allowed for the `View` class. To allow other methods, a class variable containing the list of named methods must be added:

```
class GenericView(View):
    methods = ['GET', 'POST']
    ...
    def dispatch_request(self):
        if request.method == 'GET':
            return render_template(self.template)
        elif request.method == 'POST':
            ...
```

Method class views

Often, when functions handle multiple HTTP methods, the code can become difficult to read due to large sections of code nested within `if` statements:

```python
@app.route('/user', methods=['GET', 'POST', 'PUT', 'DELETE'])
def users():
    if request.method == 'GET':
        ...
    elif request.method == 'POST':
        ...
    elif request.method == 'PUT':
        ...
    elif request.method == 'DELETE':
        ...
```

This can be solved with the `MethodView` class. `MethodView` allows each method to be handled by a different class method to separate concerns:

```python
from flask.views import MethodView

class UserView(MethodView):
    def get(self):
        ...
    def post(self):
        ...
    def put(self):
        ...
    def delete(self):
        ...

app.add_url_rule(
    '/user',
    view_func=UserView.as_view('user')
)
```

Blueprints

In Flask, a **blueprint** is a method of extending an existing Flask app. Blueprints provide a way of combining groups of views with common functionality and allow developers to break their app down into different components. In our architecture, blueprints will act as our *controllers*.

Views are registered to a blueprint; a separate template and static folder can be defined for it, and when it has all the desired content on it, it can be registered on the main Flask app to add blueprint content. A blueprint acts much like a Flask app object, but is not actually a self-contained app. This is how Flask extensions provide view functions. To get an idea of what blueprints are, here is a very simple example:

```
from flask import Blueprint
example = Blueprint(
    'example',
    __name__,
    template_folder='templates/example',
    static_folder='static/example',
    url_prefix="/example"
)

@example.route('/')
def home():
    return render_template('home.html')
```

The blueprint takes two required parameters—the name of the blueprint and the name of the package—that are used internally in Flask; passing `__name__` to it will suffice.

The other parameters are optional and define where the blueprint will look for files. Because `templates_folder` was specified, the blueprint will not look in the default template folder, and the route will render `templates/example/home.html` and not `templates/home.html`. The `url_prefix` option automatically adds the provided URI to the start of every route in the blueprint. So, the URL for the home view is actually `/example/`.

The `url_for()` function will now have to be told which blueprint the requested route is in:

```
{{ url_for('example.home') }}
```

Also, the `url_for()` function will now have to be told whether the view is being rendered from within the same blueprint:

```
{{ url_for('.home') }}
```

The `url_for()` function will also look for static files in the specified static folder.

To add the blueprint to our app:

```
app.register_blueprint(example)
```

Let's transform our current app to one that uses blueprints. We will first need to define our blueprint before all of our routes:

```
blog_blueprint = Blueprint(
    'blog',
    __name__,
    template_folder='templates/blog',
    url_prefix="/blog"
)
```

Now, because the templates folder was defined, we need to move all of our templates into a subfolder of the templates folder named blog. Next, all of our routes need to have the @app.route changed to @blog_blueprint.route, and any class view assignments now need to be registered to blog_blueprint. Remember that url_for() function calls in the templates will also have to be changed to have a period prepended to then to indicate that the route is in the same blueprint.

At the end of the file, right before the if __name__ == '__main__': statement, add the following:

```
app.register_blueprint(blog_blueprint)
```

Now all of our content is back on the app, which is registered under the blueprint. Because our base app no longer has any views, let's add a redirect on the base URL:

```
@app.route('/')
def index():
    return redirect(url_for('blog.home'))
```

Why blog and not blog_blueprint? Because blog is the name of the blueprint and the name is what Flask uses internally for routing. blog_blueprint is the name of the variable in the Python file.

Summary

We now have our app working inside a blueprint, but what does this give us? Let's say that we wanted to add a photo sharing function to our site; we would be able to group all the view functions into one blueprint with its own templates, static folder, and URL prefix without any fear of disrupting the functionality of the rest of the site. In the next chapter, blueprints will be made even more powerful by separating them into different files after upgrading our file and code structure.

5
Advanced Application Structure

Our application has gone from a very simple example to an extendable foundation on which powerful features can easily be built. However, having our application entirely resided in one file needlessly clutters our code. To make the application code clearer and more comprehensible, we will transform the entire code into a Python module and split the code into multiple files.

The project as a module

Currently, your folder structure should look like this:

```
webapp/
  config.py
  database.db
  main.py
  manage.py
  env/
  migrations/
    versions/
  static/
    css/
    js/
  templates/
    blog/
```

To convert our code to a module, our files will be converted to this folder structure:

```
webapp/
  manage.py
  database.db
  webapp/
    __init__.py
    config.py
    forms.py
    models.py
    controllers/
      __init__.py
      blog.py
    static/
      css/
      js/
    templates/
      blog/
  migrations/
    versions/
```

We will create this folder structure step by step. The first change to make is to create a folder in your application that will hold the module. In this example, it will be called webapp, but can be called anything except a blog, because the controllers are called blogs. If there are two blog objects to import from, Python will not import objects correctly from the parent directory while importing inside the blog.py file.

Next move main.py and config.py—the static and template folders, respectively— into your project folder and create a controllers folder as well. We will also need to create the files forms.py and models.py in the project folder, and a blog.py file in the controllers folder. Also, the main.py file will need to be renamed __init__.py.

The filename __init__.py looks odd, but it has a specific function. In Python, a folder can be marked as a module by placing a file named __init__.py inside it. This allows programs to import objects and variables from the Python files in the folder.

To learn more about organizing Python code in a module, refer to the official documentation at https://docs.python.org/2/ tutorial/modules.html#packages.

Refactoring the code

Let's begin moving our SQLAlchemy code to the `models.py` file. Cut all the model declarations, the table of tags, and the database object from `__init__.py` and copy them to the `models.py` file along with the SQLAlchemy import. Also, our `db` object will no longer be initialized with the `app` object as a parameter because the `app` object is not present in the `models.py` file, and importing it would result in a cyclical import. Instead, we will have the `app` object added on to the `db` object after our models are initialized. This will be achieved later in our `__init__.py` file.

Your `models.py` file should now look like this:

```python
from flask.ext.sqlalchemy import SQLAlchemy

db = SQLAlchemy()

tags = db.Table(
    'post_tags',
    db.Column('post_id', db.Integer, db.ForeignKey('post.id')),
    db.Column('tag_id', db.Integer, db.ForeignKey('tag.id'))
)

class User(db.Model):
    ...

class Post(db.Model):
    ...

class Comment(db.Model):
    ...

class Tag(db.Model):
    ...
```

Next, the `CommentForm` object, along with all the WTForms imports, should be moved to the `forms.py` file. The `forms.py` file will hold all the WTForms objects in their own file.

The `forms.py` file should look like this:

```python
from flask_wtf import Form
from wtforms import StringField, TextAreaField
from wtforms.validators import DataRequired, Length


class CommentForm(Form):
    ...
```

The `blog_blueprint` data function, all its routes, and the `sidebar_data` data function need to be moved to the `blog.py` file in the controllers folder.

The `blog.py` file should now look like this:

```
import datetime
from os import path
from sqlalchemy import func
from flask import render_template, Blueprint

from webapp.models import db, Post, Tag, Comment, User, tags
from webapp.forms import CommentForm

blog_blueprint = Blueprint(
    'blog',
    __name__,
    template_folder=path.join(path.pardir, 'templates', 'blog')
    url_prefix="/blog"
)

def sidebar_data():
    ...
```

Now, whenever a new blueprint is made, a new file in the controllers folder can be made for it, breaking down the application code into logical groups. Also, we need an empty __init__.py file in the controllers folder in order to mark it as a module.

Finally, we focus on our __init__.py file. All that should remain in the __init__.py file is the app object creation, the index route, and the blog_blueprint registration on the app object. However, there is one thing to add — the database initialization. With the db.init_app() function, we will add the app object to the db object after it's imported:

```
from flask import Flask, redirect, url_for
from config import DevConfig

from models import db
from controllers.blog import blog_blueprint

app = Flask(__name__)
app.config.from_object(DevConfig)

db.init_app(app)

@app.route('/')
def index():
    return redirect(url_for('blog.home'))

app.register_blueprint(blog_blueprint)

if __name__ == '__main__':
    app.run()
```

There are two final things to fix before our new structure works if you are using SQLite—the SQLAlchemy database URL in `config.py` needs to be updated and the imports in `manage.py` need to be updated. Because the SQLAlchemy URL for a SQLite database is a relative file path, it has to be changed to:

```
from os import path

class DevConfig(object):
    SQLALCHEMY_DATABASE_URI = 'sqlite://' + path.join(
        path.pardir,
        'database.db'
    )
```

To fix the `manage.py` imports, replace the imports from `main.py` with:

```
from webapp import app
from webapp.models import db, User, Post, Tag, Comment
```

Now if you run `manage.py` file, your app will run with the new structure.

Application factories

Now that we are using blueprints in a modular manner, however, there is another improvement we can make to our abstraction, which creates a **factory** for our application. The concept of a factory comes from the **object-oriented programming (OOP)** world, and it simply means a function or an object that creates another object. Our application factory will take one of our `config` objects, which we created at the beginning of the book and returned a Flask application object.

> The object factory design was popularized by the now famous book, *Design Patterns: Elements of Reusable Object-Oriented Software*, by the Gang of Four. To learn more about these design patterns and how they can help simplify a project's code, look at https://en.wikipedia.org/wiki/Structural_pattern.

Creating a factory function for our application object has several benefits. First, it allows the context of the environment to change the configuration of the application. When your server creates the application object to serve, it can take into account any changes in the server necessary and change the configuration object given to the app accordingly. Second, it makes testing much easier because it allows differently configured applications to be tested quickly. Third, multiple instances of the same application using the same configuration can be created very easily. This is useful for situations where web traffic is balanced across several different servers.

Now that the benefits of application factories are clear, let's modify our __init__.py file to implement it:

```python
from flask import Flask, redirect, url_for
from models import db
from controllers.blog import blog_blueprint

def create_app(object_name):
    app = Flask(__name__)
    app.config.from_object(object_name)

    db.init_app(app)

    @app.route('/')
    def index():
        return redirect(url_for('blog.home'))

    app.register_blueprint(blog_blueprint)

    return app
```

The change to the file is very simple; we contained our code in a function that takes a config object and returns an application object. We will need to modify our manage.py file in order to work with the create_app function as follows:

```python
import os
from flask.ext.script import Manager, Server
from flask.ext.migrate import Migrate, MigrateCommand
from webapp import create_app
from webapp.models import db, User, Post, Tag, Comment

# default to dev config
env = os.environ.get('WEBAPP_ENV', 'dev')
app = create_app('webapp.config.%sConfig' % env.capitalize())
...
manager = Manager(app)
manager.add_command("server", Server())
```

When we created our configuration objects it was mentioned that the environment that the application is running in could change the configuration of the application. This code has a very simple example of that functionality where an environment variable is loaded and determines which config object to give to the create_app function. Environment variables are **global variables** in Bash that can be accessed by many different programs. They can be set in Bash with the following syntax:

```bash
$ export WEBAPP_ENV="dev"
```

To read a variable:

```
$ echo $WEBAPP_ENV
dev
```

You can also delete the variable easily as follows:

```
$ unset $WEBAPP_ENV
$ echo $WEBAPP_ENV
```

On your production server, you would set `WEBAPP_ENV` to `prod`. The true power of this setup will become clearer once you deploy to production in *Chapter 13, Deploying Flask Apps,* and when we get to *Chapter 12, Testing Flask Apps,* which covers testing our project.

Summary

We have transformed our application into a much more manageable and scalable structure, which will save us a lot of headaches as we move further through the book and add more advanced features. In the next chapter, we will add a login and registration system to our application, and other features to make our site more secure.

6
Securing Your App

We have a mostly functioning blog app, but it is missing some crucial features, such as user login, registration, and adding and editing posts from the browser. The user login functionality can be created in many different ways, so each of the sections demonstrates mutually exclusive methods to create logins. The first way is directly using the browser's cookies, and the second way is using a Flask extension named **Flask Login**.

Setting up

Before we jump right into making a user authentication system, there is a lot of setup code. To run any type of authentication, our app will need the following elements common to all:

- First, the user models will need proper password hashing

- Second, a login form and a registration form will be needed to validate user input

- Third, a login view and a registration view with templates for each will be needed

- Fourth, various social logins need to be set up in order to tie them into the login system when it is implemented

Updating the models

Until now, our users had their passwords stored as a plain text in the database. This is a major security flaw. If any malicious user were to gain access to the data in the database, they could log in to any account. The fallout of such a breach would be greater than our site. Large amounts of people on the Internet use a common password for many sites.

If an attacker had access to an e-mail and password combination, it is very likely that this information could be used to log in to a Facebook account or even a bank account.

To protect our user passwords, they will be encrypted with a one-way encryption method named a **hashing algorithm**. A one-way encryption means that after information is encrypted, the original information cannot be regained from the result. However, given the same data, the hashing algorithm will always produce the same result. The data given to the hashing algorithm can be anything from a text file to a movie file. In this case, the data is just a string of characters. With this functionality, our passwords can be stored as **hashes** (data that has been hashed). Then, when a user enters their password in the login or registration page, the text entered for the password will be sent through the same hashing algorithm, and the stored hash and the entered hash will be verified.

There are many hashing algorithms, most of which are not secure because they are easy to **brute force**. Hackers continuously try sending data through a hashing algorithm until something matches. To best protect the user passwords, bcrypt will be our hashing algorithm of choice. **Bcrypt** is purposely designed to be inefficient and slow (milliseconds vs. microseconds) for the computer to process, thereby making it harder to brute force. To add bcrypt to our project, the package **Flask Bcrypt** will need to be installed as follows:

```
$ pip install Flask-Bcrypt
```

This is the second Flask extension that will be initialized on the app object, the other being the SQLAlchemy object. The db object was stored in the models.py file, but there is no obvious place to initialize Flask Bcrypt. To hold all future extensions, add the file named extensions.py in the same directory as the __init__.py file. Inside, Flask Bcrypt will have to be initialized:

```
from flask.ext.bcrypt import Bcrypt
bcrypt = Bcrypt()
```

It is then added to the app object:

```
from webapp.extensions import bcrypt

def create_app(object_name):
    app = Flask(__name__)
    app.config.from_object(object_name)

    db.init_app(app)
    bcrypt.init_app(app)
```

Bcrypt is now ready to use. To have our `User` object use bcrypt, we will add two methods that set the password and check if a string matches the stored hash:

```
from webapp.extensions import bcrypt

class User(db.Model):
    id = db.Column(db.Integer(), primary_key=True)
    username = db.Column(db.String(255))
    password = db.Column(db.String(255))
    posts = db.relationship(
        'Post',
        backref='user',
        lazy='dynamic'
    )

    def __init__(self, username):
        self.username = username

    def __repr__(self):
        return '<User {}>'.format(self.username)

    def set_password(self, password):
        self.password = bcrypt.generate_password_hash(password)

    def check_password(self, password):
        return bcrypt.check_password_hash(self.password, password)
```

Now, our `User` models can store passwords securely. Next, our login process needs to use these methods to create new users and check passwords.

Creating the forms

Three forms are required: a login form, a registration form, and a form for our **post creation** page. The login form will have username and password fields:

```
from wtforms import (
    StringField,
    TextAreaField,
    PasswordField,
    BooleanField
)
from wtforms.validators import DataRequired, Length, EqualTo, URL

class LoginForm(Form):
    username = StringField('Username', [
        DataRequired(), Length(max=255)
    ])
```

```
    password = PasswordField('Password', [DataRequired()])

def validate(self):
    check_validate = super(LoginForm, self).validate()

    # if our validators do not pass
    if not check_validate:
        return False

    # Does our the exist
    user = User.query.filter_by(
        username=self.username.data
    ).first()
    if not user:
        self.username.errors.append(
            'Invalid username or password'
        )
        return False

    # Do the passwords match
    if not self.user.check_password(self.password.data):
        self.username.errors.append(
            'Invalid username or password'
        )
        return False

    return True
```

Along with the normal validations, our `LoginForm` method will also check whether the username passed exists and will use the `check_password()` method to check the hashes.

Protecting your form from spam with reCAPTCHA

The registration form will have a username field, a password field with a confirmation field, and a special field named a reCAPTCHA field. A CAPTCHA is a special field on a web form that checks whether whoever is entering data into the form is actually a person, or an automated program that is spamming your site. reCAPTCHA is simply one implementation of a CAPTCHA. reCAPTCHA has been integrated into WTForms as it is the most popular implementation on the Web.

To use reCAPTCHA, you will need a reCAPTCHA login from https://www. google.com/recaptcha/intro/index.html. As reCAPTCHA is a Google product, you can log in with your Google account.

Once you log in, it will ask you to add a site. In this case, any name will do, but the domain field must have `localhost` as an entry. Once you deploy your site, your domain must also be added to this list.

Now that you have added a site, dropdowns with instructions on server and client integration will appear. The given `script` tag will need to be added to the templates of our login and registration views when we create them. What WTForms needs from this page are the keys, as shown in the following screenshot:

Remember to never show these keys to public. As these keys are only registered to `localhost`, they can be shown here without recourse.

Add these keys to the `config` object in the `config.py` file so that WTForms can access them as follows:

```
class Config(object):
    SECRET_KEY = 'Key Here'
    RECAPTCHA_PUBLIC_KEY =
"6LdKkQQTAAAAAEH0GFj7NLg5tGicaoOus7G9Q5Uw"
    RECAPTCHA_PRIVATE_KEY =
'6LdKkQQTAAAAAMYroksPTJ7pWhobYb88fTAcxcYn'
```

The following is our registration form:

```
class RegisterForm(Form):
    username = StringField('Username', [
        DataRequired(),
        Length(max=255)
    ])
    password = PasswordField('Password', [
        DataRequired(),
        Length(min=8)
    ])
    confirm = PasswordField('Confirm Password', [
        DataRequired(),
        EqualTo('password')
    ])
```

```
    recaptcha = RecaptchaField()

    def validate(self):
        check_validate = super(RegisterForm, self).validate()

        # if our validators do not pass
        if not check_validate:
            return False

        user = User.query.filter_by(
            username=self.username.data
        ).first()

        # Is the username already being used
        if user:
            self.username.errors.append(
                "User with that name already exists"
            )
            return False

        return True
```

The post creation form will just contain a text input for the title and a text area input for the post content:

```
class PostForm(Form):
    title = StringField('Title', [
        DataRequired(),
        Length(max=255)
    ])
    text = TextAreaField('Content', [DataRequired()])
```

Creating views

In the previous chapter, the index view containing the redirect to the blog home was stored in the `create_app` function. That was alright for one view. Now, this section is going to add many views on the base URL of the site. As such, we need a new controller in `controllers/main.py`:

```
main_blueprint = Blueprint(
    'main',
    __name__,
```

```
        template_folder='../templates/main'
)


@main_blueprint.route('/')
def index():
    return redirect(url_for('blog.home'))
```

The login and registration views will create our form objects and pass them to the templates. For now, the login form will not do anything if the data passed validates. The actual login functionality will be added in the next section. However, the registration view will create a new user if the data passes validation. Along with the login and registration views, there needs to be a logout view, which will do nothing for now as well.

In the main.py controller, add the following:

```
from webapp.forms import LoginForm, RegisterForm


@main_blueprint.route('/login', methods=['GET', 'POST'])
def login():
    form = LoginForm()

    if form.validate_on_submit():
        flash("You have been logged in.", category="success")
        return redirect(url_for('blog.home'))

    return render_template('login.html', form=form)

@main_blueprint.route('/logout', methods=['GET', 'POST'])
def logout():
    flash("You have been logged out.", category="success")
    return redirect(url_for('.home'))

@main_blueprint.route('/register', methods=['GET', 'POST'])
def register():
    form = RegisterForm()

    if form.validate_on_submit():
        new_user = User()
        new_user.username = form.username.data
        new_user.set_password(form.username.data)
```

```
        db.session.add(new_user)
        db.session.commit()

        flash(
            "Your user has been created, please login.",
            category="success"
        )

        return redirect(url_for('.login'))

    return render_template('register.html', form=form)
```

The `login.html` and `register.html` templates used in the preceding code (placed in the `templates/main` folder) can be made with the `form` macro created in *Chapter 3, Creating Views with Templates*, but the `script` tag from reCAPTCHA cannot be added to `register.html` yet.

First, there needs to be a way for our child templates to add new JavaScript files to the `base.html` template. There also needs to be a way for our views to flash messages to the user with the Flask `flash` function. A new content block has to be added to the `base.html` file along with a loop over the messages:

```html
<body>
  <div class="container">
    <div class="jumbotron">
      <h1><a href="{{ url_for('blog.home') }}">My Blog</a></h1>
      <p>Welcome to the blog!</p>
    </div>
    {% with messages = get_flashed_messages(with_categories=true) %}
      {% if messages %}
        {% for category, message in messages %}
          <div class="alert alert-{{ category }} alert-dismissible"
            role="alert">
          <button type="button" class="close" data-dismiss="alert"
aria-label="Close"><span aria-hidden="true">&times;</span></button>

          {{ message }}
          </div>
        {% endfor %}
      {% endif %}
    {% endwith %}
    {% block body %}
    {% endblock %}
  </div>
```

```
<script
    src="https://ajax.googleapis.com/ajax/libs/jquery/1.11.2/jquery.
min.js">
    </script>
<script
    src="https://maxcdn.bootstrapcdn.com/bootstrap/3.3.2/js/bootstrap.
min.js">
    </script>
{% block js %}
{% endblock %}
</body>
```

Your login page should now resemble the following:

Your registration page should look like this:

Now we need to create the post creation and editing page so something can be secured. The two pages will need to transform the text area field into a **WYSIWYG** (short for **What You See Is What You Get**) editor to handle wrapping the post text in HTML. In the `blog.py` controller, add the following views:

```python
from webapp.forms import CommentForm, PostForm

@blog_blueprint.route('/new', methods=['GET', 'POST'])
def new_post():
    form = PostForm()

    if form.validate_on_submit():
        new_post = Post(form.title.data)
        new_post.text = form.text.data
        new_post.publish_date = datetime.datetime.now()

        db.session.add(new_post)
        db.session.commit()

    return render_template('new.html', form=form)

@blog_blueprint.route('/edit/<int:id>', methods=['GET', 'POST'])
def edit_post(id):

    post = Post.query.get_or_404(id)
    form = PostForm()

    if form.validate_on_submit():
        post.title = form.title.data
        post.text = form.text.data
        post.publish_date = datetime.datetime.now()

        db.session.add(post)
        db.session.commit()

        return redirect(url_for('.post', post_id=post.id))

    form.text.data = post.text

    return render_template('edit.html', form=form, post=post)
```

This functionality is much like the code used to add new comments. The data of the text field is set in the view because there is no easy way to set the contents of `TextAreaField` inside a template.

The `new.html` template will need a JavaScript file for the WYSIWYG editor. **CKEditor** is very simple to install and use. Now, our `new.html` file can be created as follows:

```
{% extends "base.html" %}
{% block title %}Post Creation{% endblock %}
{% block body %}
<div class="row">
  <h1 class="text-center">Create A New Post</h1>
  <form method="POST" action="{{ url_for('.new_post') }}">
    {{ form.hidden_tag() }}
    <div class="form-group">
      {{ form.title.label }}
      {% if form.title.errors %}
        {% for e in form.title.errors %}
          <p class="help-block">{{ e }}</p>
        {% endfor %}
      {% endif %}
      {{ form.title(class_='form-control') }}
    </div>
    <div class="form-group">
      {{ form.text.label }}
      {% if form.text.errors %}
        {% for e in form.text.errors %}
          <p class="help-block">{{ e }}</p>
        {% endfor %}
      {% endif %}
      {{ form.text(id="editor", class_='form-control') }}
    </div>
    <input class="btn btn-primary" type="submit" value="Submit">
  </form>
</div>
{% endblock %}

{% block js %}
<script src="//cdn.ckeditor.com/4.4.7/standard/ckeditor.js"></script>
<script>
```

```
      CKEDITOR.replace('editor');
</script>
{% endblock %}
```

This is all that is needed to have the user's input stored as HTML in the database. Because we passed the safe filter in our post template, the HTML code appears correctly on our post pages. The `edit.html` template is similar to the `new.html` template. The only difference is the `form` opening tag and the creation of the `title` field:

```
<form method="POST" action="{{ url_for('.edit_post', id=post.id)
    }}">
...
{{ form.title(class_='form-control', value=post.title) }}
...
</form>
```

The `post.html` template will need a button for authors to link them to the edit page:

```
<div class="row">
  <div class="col-lg-6">
     <p>Written By <a href="{{ url_for('.user', username=post.user.
username)
        }}">{{ post.user.username }}</a> on {{ post.publish_date }}</p>
  </div>
  ...
  <div class="row">
    <div class="col-lg-2">
    <a href="{{ url_for('.edit_post', id=post.id) }}" class="btn btn-
      primary">Edit</a>
  </div>
</div>
```

When we are able to detect the current user, the edit button will only be shown to the user who created the post.

Social logins

Integrating alternative login and registration options into your site becomes more important as time goes on. Every month, there is another announcement that passwords have been stolen from a popular website. Implementing the following login options means that our site's database never stores a password for that user.

Verification is handled by a large brand name company, which the user already places their trust in. By using social logins, the amount of trust a user has to place in the website they are using is much lower. Your login process also becomes much shorter for the user, decreasing the barrier to entry to your app.

Socially authenticated users act as normal users, and unlike the password-based login methods, they all can be used in tandem.

OpenID

OpenID is an open protocol that allows users on one site to be authenticated by any third-party site that implements the protocol, which are called **Relaying Parties (RPs)**. An OpenID login is represented as a URL from one of the RPs, typically the profile page of the website.

 To know a full list of sites that use OpenID and how to use each, go to `http://openid.net/get-an-openid/`.

To add OpenID to Flask, a Flask extension named **Flask-OpenID** will be needed:

```
$ pip install Flask-OpenID
```

Our app will need a couple of things to implement OpenID:

* A new form object
* The form validation on the login and registration pages
* A callback after the form submission to log the user in or create a new user

In the `extensions.py` file, the OpenID object can be initialized as follows:

```
from flask.ext.bcrypt import Bcrypt
from flask.ext.openid import OpenID
bcrypt = Bcrypt()
oid = OpenID()
```

In the `__init__.py` file, the `oid` object is registered to the `app` object:

```
from .models import db

def create_app(object_name):
    app = Flask(__name__)
    app.config.from_object(object_name)
```

```
db.init_app(app)
bcrypt.init_app(app)
oid.init_app(app)
```

The new `form` object will only need the URL of the RP:

```
from wtforms.validators import DataRequired, Length, EqualTo, URL

class OpenIDForm(Form):
    openid = StringField('OpenID URL', [DataRequired(), URL()])
```

On the login and registration views, `OpenIDForm()` will be initialized, and if the data is valid, a login request will be sent:

```
from webapp.extensions import oid
...


@main_blueprint.route('/login', methods=['GET', 'POST'])
@oid.loginhandler
def login():
    form = LoginForm()
    openid_form = OpenIDForm()

    if openid_form.validate_on_submit():
        return oid.try_login(
            openid_form.openid.data,
            ask_for=['nickname', 'email'],
            ask_for_optional=['fullname']
        )

    if form.validate_on_submit():
        flash("You have been logged in.", category="success")
        return redirect(url_for('blog.home'))

    openid_errors = oid.fetch_error()
    if openid_errors:
        flash(openid_errors, category="danger")

    return render_template(
        'login.html',
        form=form,
        openid_form=openid_form
    )
```

```python
@main_blueprint.route('/register', methods=['GET', 'POST'])
@oid.loginhandler
def register():
    form = RegisterForm()
    openid_form = OpenIDForm()

    if openid_form.validate_on_submit():
        return oid.try_login(
            openid_form.openid.data,
            ask_for=['nickname', 'email'],
            ask_for_optional=['fullname']
        )

    if form.validate_on_submit():
        new_user = User(form.username.data)
        new_user.set_password(form.password.data)

        db.session.add(new_user)
        db.session.commit()

        flash(
            "Your user has been created, please login.",
            category="success"
        )

        return redirect(url_for('.login'))

    openid_errors = oid.fetch_error()
    if openid_errors:
        flash(openid_errors, category="danger")

    return render_template(
        'register.html',
        form=form,
        openid_form=openid_form
    )
```

Both the views have the new decorator `@oid.loginhandler`, which tells Flask-OpenID to listen for authentication information coming back from the RP. With OpenID, logging in and registering are the same. It is possible to create a user from the login form and to log in from the registration form. The same field appears on both pages to avoid user confusion.

To handle the user creation and login, a new function in the `extensions.py` file is needed:

```
@oid.after_login
def create_or_login(resp):
    from models import db, User
    username = resp.fullname or resp.nickname or resp.email
    if not username:
        flash('Invalid login. Please try again.', 'danger')
        return redirect(url_for('main.login'))

    user = User.query.filter_by(username=username).first()
    if user is None:
        user = User(username)
        db.session.add(user)
        db.session.commit()

    # Log the user in here
    return redirect(url_for('blog.home'))
```

This function is called after every successful response from the RP. If the login is successful and a user object does not exist for the identity, this function creates a new `User` object. If one already exists, the upcoming authentication methods will log the user in. OpenID does not require all possible information to be returned, so it is possible that rather than a full name, only an e-mail will be returned. This is why the username can be the nickname, full name, or e-mail. The `db` and `User` object are imported inside the function to avoid cyclical imports from the `models.py` file importing the `bcrypt` object.

Facebook

To log in with Facebook, and later Twitter, a protocol named **OAuth** is used. Our app will not use OAuth directly, instead another Flask extension will be used named **Flask OAuth**:

```
$ pip install Flask-OAuth
```

To use Facebook login, our app needs to define a Facebook OAuth object with our app's keys. Define a view that redirects the user to the login authorization process on Facebook's server, and a function on the Facebook method to load the `auth` token from the login process.

First, a Facebook app needs to be created at `http://developers.facebook.com`. Once you create a new app, look for the panel that lists your app's id and secret key.

Use these values while adding the following code to `extensions.py`:

```python
from flask_oauth import OAuth

bcrypt = Bcrypt()
oid = OpenID()
oauth = OAuth()

...

facebook = oauth.remote_app(
    'facebook',
    base_url='https://graph.facebook.com/',
    request_token_url=None,
    access_token_url='/oauth/access_token',
    authorize_url='https://www.facebook.com/dialog/oauth',
    consumer_key=' FACEBOOK_APP_ID',
    consumer_secret=' FACEBOOK_APP_SECRET',
    request_token_params={'scope': 'email'}
)
@facebook.tokengetter
def get_facebook_oauth_token():
    return session.get('facebook_oauth_token')
```

In the Facebook developer interface, be sure to add a new authorized website as `http://localhost:5000/` or the login will not work. In the `main.py` controller, add the following code:

```python
from webapp.extensions import oid, facebook
...

@main_blueprint.route('/facebook')
def facebook_login():
    return facebook.authorize(
        callback=url_for(
            '.facebook_authorized',
            next=request.referrer or None,
            _external=True
        )
    )


@main_blueprint.route('/facebook/authorized')
@facebook.authorized_handler
def facebook_authorized(resp):
    if resp is None:
        return 'Access denied: reason=%s error=%s' % (
            request.args['error_reason'],
            request.args['error_description']
        )

    session['facebook_oauth_token'] = (resp['access_token'], '')

    me = facebook.get('/me')
    user = User.query.filter_by(
        username=me.data['first_name'] + " " + me.data['last_name']
    ).first()

    if not user:
        user = User(me.data['first_name'] + " " + me.data['last_
name'])
        db.session.add(user)
        db.session.commit()

    # Login User here
```

```
flash("You have been logged in.", category="success")

return redirect(
    request.args.get('next') or url_for('blog.home')
)
```

The first route, `facebook_login`, is just a redirect to the login process on Facebook's website. The `facebook_authorized` view receives the response from Facebook's servers and, just like the OpenID process, either creates a new user or logs the user in. Now to start the process, add the following link to the registration and login templates:

```
<h2 class="text-center">Register With Facebook</h2>
<a href="{{ url_for('.facebook_login') }}">Login via Facebook</a>
```

Twitter

The Twitter login process is very similar. To create a Twitter app and receive your keys, go to `https://apps.twitter.com/`. In `extensions.py`:

```
twitter = oauth.remote_app(
    'twitter',
    base_url='https://api.twitter.com/1.1/',
    request_token_url='https://api.twitter.com/oauth/request_token',
    access_token_url='https://api.twitter.com/oauth/access_token',
    authorize_url='https://api.twitter.com/oauth/authenticate',
    consumer_key='',
    consumer_secret=''
)


@twitter.tokengetter
def get_twitter_oauth_token():
    return session.get('twitter_oauth_token')
```

In the `main.py` controller, add the following views:

```
@main_blueprint.route('/twitter-login')
def twitter_login():
    return twitter.authorize(
        callback=url_for(
            '.twitter_authorized',
            next=request.referrer or None,
            _external=True
        )
    )
```

```
@main_blueprint.route('/twitter-login/authorized')
@twitter.authorized_handler
def twitter_authorized(resp):
    if resp is None:
        return 'Access denied: reason: {} error: {}'.format(
            request.args['error_reason'],
            request.args['error_description']
        )

    session['twitter_oauth_token'] = resp['oauth_token'] + \
        resp['oauth_token_secret']

    user = User.query.filter_by(
        username=resp['screen_name']
    ).first()

    if not user:
        user = User(resp['screen_name'], '')
        db.session.add(user)
        db.session.commit()

    # Login User here
    flash("You have been logged in.", category="success")

    return redirect(
        request.args.get('next') or url_for('blog.home')
    )
```

These views perform the same function as their Facebook counterparts. Finally, in the register and login templates, add the following link to start the login process:

```
<h2 class="text-center">Register With Twitter</h2>
<a href="{{ url_for('.twitter_login') }}">Login</a>
```

Using the session

One way to create authentication in Flask is to use the `session` object. The `session` object is an object in Flask that creates an easy way for the server to store information in the user's browser with cookies. The stored data is cryptographically signed with the app's secret key. If the user attempts to modify the cookie, then the sign will no longer be valid and the cookie will not be read.

The session object has the same API as a `dict` object. To add data to it, simply use this:

```
session['key'] = data
```

To retrieve data, use this:

```
session['key']
```

To log a user in, a username key will be added to the session and set to the username of the current user.

```
@main_blueprint.route('/login', methods=['GET', 'POST'])
def login():
    form = LoginForm()

    if form.validate_on_submit():
        # Add the user's name to the cookie
        session['username'] = form.username.data

    return render_template('login.html', form=form)
```

To log the user out, the key can be popped from the session:

```
@main_blueprint.route('/logout', methods=['GET', 'POST'])
def logout():
    # Remove the username from the cookie
    session.pop('username', None)
    return redirect(url_for('.login'))
```

To check whether a user is currently logged in, the view can test if the username key exists in the session. Consider the following new post view:

```
@blog_blueprint.route('/new', methods=['GET', 'POST'])
def new_post ():
    if 'username' not in session:
        return redirect(url_for('main.login'))
    ...
```

Some of our templates will need access to the current user object. At the start of every request, our `blog` blueprint can check whether the username is in the session. If so, add the `User` object to the `g` object, which is accessible through the templates.

```
@blog_blueprint.before_request
def check_user():
    if 'username' in session:
```

```
        g.current_user = User.query.filter_by(
            username=session['username']
        ).one()
    else:
        g.current_user = None
```

Our login check can be changed to:

```
@blog_blueprint.route('/new', methods=['GET', 'POST'])
def new_post():
    if not g.current_user:
        return redirect(url_for('main.login'))
    ...
```

Also, the edit button on the post page should only appear when the current user is the author:

```
{% if g.current_user == post.user %}
<div class="row">
  <div class="col-lg-2">
    <a href="{{ url_for('.edit_post', id=post.id) }}" class="btn btn-
      primary">Edit</a>
  </div>
</div>
{% endif %}
```

The edit page itself should also perform the following check:

```
@blog_blueprint.route('/edit/<int:id>', methods=['GET', 'POST'])
def edit_post(id):
    if not g.current_user:
        return redirect(url_for('main.login'))

    post = Post.query.get_or_404(id)

    if g.current_user != post.user:
        abort(403)
    ...
```

Now our app has a fully featured login system with a traditional username and password combination and many social logins as well. However, there are some features that are not covered in this system. For example, what if we wanted some users to be able to only comment while giving others permission to create posts? Also, our login system does not implement a `Remember Me` function. To cover this functionality, we will refactor our app to use a Flask extension named **Flask Login** instead of directly using the session.

Flask Login

To start using Flask Login, it needs to be downloaded first:

```
$ pip install flask-login
```

The main Flask Login object is the LoginManager object. Like the other Flask extensions, initialize the LoginManager object in extensions.py:

```
from flask.ext.login import LoginManager

...

login_manager = LoginManager()
```

There are some configuration options that need to be changed on the object:

```
login_manager.login_view = "main.login"
login_manager.session_protection = "strong"
login_manager.login_message = "Please login to access this page"
login_manager.login_message_category = "info"


@login_manager.user_loader
def load_user(userid):
    from models import User
    return User.query.get(userid)
```

The preceding configuration values define which view should be treated as the login page and what the message to the user while logging in should look like. Setting the option session_protection to strong better protects against malicious users tampering with their cookies. When a tampered cookie is identified, the session object for that user is deleted and the user is forced to log back in. The load_user function takes an id and returns the User object. It's for Flask Login to check whether an id identifies the correct user object.

The User model needs to be updated to include some methods for Flask Login. First is is_authenticated to check whether the User object has been logged in. Next is is_active, which checks whether the user has gone through some sort of activation process, such as an e-mail confirmation. Otherwise, it allows site administrators to ban a user without deleting their data. Then, is_anonymous checks whether this user is anonymous and not logged in. Finally, a get_id function returns a unique unicode identifier for that User object.

This app will use a simple implementation for this functionality:

```python
from flask.ext.login import AnonymousUserMixin
...


class User(db.Model):
    id = db.Column(db.Integer(), primary_key=True)
    username = db.Column(db.String(255))
    password = db.Column(db.String(255))
    posts = db.relationship(
        'Post',
        backref='user',
        lazy='dynamic'
    )

    def __init__(self, username):
        self.username = username

    def __repr__(self):
        return '<User {}>'.format(self.username)

    def set_password(self, password):
        self.password = bcrypt.generate_password_hash(password)

    def check_password(self, password):
        return bcrypt.check_password_hash(self.password, password)

    def is_authenticated(self):
        if isinstance(self, AnonymousUserMixin):
            return False
        else:
            return True

    def is_active(self):
        return True

    def is_anonymous(self):
        if isinstance(self, AnonymousUserMixin):
            return True
        else:
            return False

    def get_id(self):
        return unicode(self.id)
```

In Flask Login, every user on the site inherits from some user object. By default, they inherit an `AnonymousUserMixin` object. If your site needs some functionality with anonymous users, you can create a class that inherits from `AnonymousUserMixin` and set it as the default user class with the following:

```
login_manager.anonymous_user = CustomAnonymousUser
```

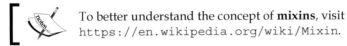 To better understand the concept of **mixins**, visit `https://en.wikipedia.org/wiki/Mixin`.

To log in a user with Flask Login, use:

```
from flask.ext.login import login_user
login_user(user_object)
```

Flask Login then takes care of all of the session handling. To have the user be remembered, add `remember=True,` to the `login_user` call. A checkbox can be added to the login form to give users the choice:

```
from wtforms import (
    StringField,
    TextAreaField,
    PasswordField,
    BooleanField
)

class LoginForm(Form):
    username = StringField('Username', [
        DataRequired(),
        Length(max=255)
    ])
    password = PasswordField('Password', [DataRequired()])
    remember = BooleanField("Remember Me")
    ...
```

In the login view, add this:

```
if form.validate_on_submit():
    user = User.query.filter_by(
        username=form.username.data
    ).one()
    login_user(user, remember=form.remember.data)
```

To log the current user out, use the following:

```
from flask.ext.login import login_user, logout_user
logout_user()
```

To protect a view from unauthorized users and send them to the login page, add the login_required decorator as follows:

```
from flask.ext.login import login_required

@blog_blueprint.route('/new', methods=['GET', 'POST'])
@login_required
def new_post():
    form = PostForm()
    ...
```

Flask Login also provides a proxy to the logged in user with current_user. This proxy is available in views and templates alike. So, in our blog controller, the custom before_request handler can be deleted, and our calls to g.current_user should be replaced with current_user.

Now, with Flask Login, our app's login system is more Pythonic and secure. There is one last feature to implement: user roles and permissions.

User roles

To add user permissions to our application, our User model will need a many-to-many relationship to a Role object, and it will need another Flask extension named **Flask Principal**.

With our code from *Chapter 2, Creating Models with SQLAlchemy*, adding a many-to-many relationship to the User object is easy:

```
roles = db.Table(
    'role_users',
    db.Column('user_id', db.Integer, db.ForeignKey('user.id')),
    db.Column('role_id', db.Integer, db.ForeignKey('role.id'))
)

class User(db.Model):
    id = db.Column(db.Integer(), primary_key=True)
```

```
        username = db.Column(db.String(255), unique=True)
        password = db.Column(db.String(255))
        posts = db.relationship(
            'Post',
            backref='user',
            lazy='dynamic'
        )
        roles = db.relationship(
            'Role',
            secondary=roles,
            backref=db.backref('users', lazy='dynamic')
        )

        def __init__(self, username):
            self.username = username

            default = Role.query.filter_by(name="default").one()
            self.roles.append(default)
        ...

class Role(db.Model):
    id = db.Column(db.Integer(), primary_key=True)
    name = db.Column(db.String(80), unique=True)
    description = db.Column(db.String(255))

    def __init__(self, name):
        self.name = name

    def __repr__(self):
        return '<Role {}>'.format(self.name)
```

From the command line, populate the roles table with three roles: admin, poster, and default. These will act as the main permissions for Flask Principal.

Flask Principal works around the idea of an identity. Something in the application, a User object in our case, has an identity associated with it. The identity provides Need objects, which at their core are just named tuples. Needs define what the identity can do. Permissions are initialized with Need, and they define what Need objects a resource needs to be accessed.

Flask Principal provides two convenient `Need` objects: `UserNeed` and `RoleNeed`, which are exactly what is needed for our app. In `extensions.py`, Flask Principal will be initialized and our `RoleNeed` objects will be created:

```
from flask.ext.principal import Principal, Permission, RoleNeed
principals = Principal()
admin_permission = Permission(RoleNeed('admin'))
poster_permission = Permission(RoleNeed('poster'))
default_permission = Permission(RoleNeed('default'))
```

Flask Principal requires a function that adds `Need` objects to it after the identity has changed. Because this function requires access to the `app` object, this function will reside in the `__init__.py` file:

```
from flask.ext.principal import identity_loaded, UserNeed, RoleNeed
from extensions import bcrypt, oid, login_manager, principals
def create_app(object_name):
    app = Flask(__name__)
    app.config.from_object(object_name)

    db.init_app(app)
    bcrypt.init_app(app)
    oid.init_app(app)
    login_manager.init_app(app)
    principals.init_app(app)

    @identity_loaded.connect_via(app)
    def on_identity_loaded(sender, identity):
        # Set the identity user object
        identity.user = current_user

        # Add the UserNeed to the identity
        if hasattr(current_user, 'id'):
            identity.provides.add(UserNeed(current_user.id))

        # Add each role to the identity
        if hasattr(current_user, 'roles'):
            for role in current_user.roles:
                identity.provides.add(RoleNeed(role.name))
    ...
```

Now when the identity is changed, it will add a `UserNeed` and all of the `RoleNeed` objects as well. The identity changes when the user logs in or logs out:

```python
from flask.ext.principal import (
    Identity,
    AnonymousIdentity,
    identity_changed
)
@main_blueprint.route('/login', methods=['GET', 'POST'])
@oid.loginhandler
def login():
    ...

    if form.validate_on_submit():
        user = User.query.filter_by(
            username=form.username.data
        ).one()
        login_user(user, remember=form.remember.data)

        identity_changed.send(
            current_app._get_current_object(),
            identity=Identity(user.id)
        )

        flash("You have been logged in.", category="success")
        return redirect(url_for('blog.home'))
@main_blueprint.route('/logout', methods=['GET', 'POST'])
def logout():
    logout_user()

    identity_changed.send(
        current_app._get_current_object(),
        identity=AnonymousIdentity()
    )

    flash("You have been logged out.", category="success")
    return redirect(url_for('.login'))
```

When the user logs in, their identity will trigger the `on_identity_loaded` method, and set their `Need` objects up. Now if we had a page that we wanted only posters to have access to:

```python
from webapp.extensions import poster_permission
@blog_blueprint.route('/edit/<int:id>', methods=['GET', 'POST'])
@login_required
@poster_permission.require(http_exception=403)
def edit_post(id):
    ...
```

We could also replace our user check in the same view with a `UserNeed` check as follows:

```python
from webapp.extensions import poster_permission, admin_permission

@blog_blueprint.route('/edit/<int:id>', methods=['GET', 'POST'])
@login_required
@poster_permission.require(http_exception=403)
def edit_post(id):
    post = Post.query.get_or_404(id)
    permission = Permission(UserNeed(post.user.id))

    # We want admins to be able to edit any post
    if permission.can() or admin_permission.can():
        form = PostForm()

        if form.validate_on_submit():
            post.title = form.title.data
            post.text = form.text.data
            post.publish_date = datetime.datetime.now()

            db.session.add(post)
            db.session.commit()

            return redirect(url_for('.post', post_id=post.id))

        form.text.data = post.text
        return render_template('edit.html', form=form, post=post)

    abort(403)
```

 Visit the documentation of Flask Principal at `https://pythonhosted.org/Flask-Principal/` to understand how to create much more complex `Need` objects.

Summary

Our users now have secure logins, multiple login and registration options, and explicit access permissions. Our app has everything that is needed to be a full-fledged blog app. In the next chapter, the book will stop following this example application in order to introduce a technology called **NoSQL**.

7
Using NoSQL with Flask

A **NoSQL** (short for **Not Only SQL**) database is any nonrelational data store. It usually focuses on speed and scalability. NoSQL has been taking the web development world by storm for the past 7 years. Huge companies, such as Netflix and Google, announced that they were moving many of their services to NoSQL databases, and many smaller companies followed this.

This chapter will deviate from the rest of the book in which Flask will not be the main focus. The focus on database design might seem odd in a book about Flask, but choosing the correct database for your application is arguably the most important decision while designing your technology stack. In the vast majority of web applications, the database is the bottleneck, so the database you pick will determine the overall speed of your app. A study conducted by Amazon showed that even a 100-ms delay caused a 1 percent reduction in sales, so speed should always be one of the main concerns of a web developer. Also, there is an abundance of horror stories in the programmer community of web developers about choosing a popular NoSQL database and then not really understanding what the database required in terms of administration. This leads to large amounts of data loss and crashes, which in turn means losing customers. All in all, it's no exaggeration to say that your choice of database for your application can be the difference between your app succeeding or failing.

To illustrate the strengths and weaknesses of NoSQL databases, each type of NoSQL database will be examined, and the differences between NoSQL and traditional databases will be laid out.

Types of NoSQL databases

NoSQL is a blanket term used to describe nontraditional methods of storing data in a database. To make matters more confusing, NoSQL may also mean the databases that are relational but did not use SQL as a query language, for example, **RethinkDB**. The vast majority of NoSQL databases are not relational, unlike RDBMS, which means that they cannot perform operations such as JOIN. The lack of a JOIN operation is a trade-off because it allows faster reads and easier decentralization by spreading data across several servers or even separate data centers.

Modern NoSQL databases include key-value stores, document stores, column family stores, and graph databases.

Key-value stores

A **key-value** NoSQL database acts much like a dictionary in Python. A single value is associated with one key and is accessed via that key. Also, like a Python dictionary, most key-value databases have the same read speed regardless of how many entries there are. Advanced programmers would know this as **O(1) reads**. In some key-value stores, only one key can be retrieved at a time, rather than multiple rows in traditional SQL databases. In most key-value stores, the content of the value is not *queryable*, but the keys are. Values are just binary blobs; they can be literally anything from a string to a movie file. However, some key-value stores give default types, such as strings, lists, sets, and dictionaries, while still giving the option of adding binary data.

Because of their simplicity, key-value stores are typically very fast. However, their simplicity makes them unsuitable as the main database for most applications. As such, most key-value store use cases are storing simple objects that need to expire after a given amount of time. Two common examples of this pattern are storing user's session data and shopping cart data. Also, key-value stores are commonly used as caches for the application or for other databases. For example, results from a commonly run, or CPU-intensive, query or function are stored with the query or function name as a key. The application will check the cache in the key-value store before running the query on the database, thereby decreasing page load times and stress on the database. An example of this functionality will be shown in *Chapter 10, Useful Flask Extensions*.

The most popular key-value stores are **Redis**, **Riak**, and **Amazon DynamoDB**.

Document stores

Document store is one of the most popular NoSQL database types and what typically replaces an RDBMS. Databases store data in collections of key-value pairs called documents. These documents are schema-less, meaning no document must follow the structure of another document. Also, extra keys may be appended to the document after its creation. Most document stores store data in **JSON (JavaScript Object Notation)**, a superset of JSON, or XML. For example, the following are two different post objects stored in JSON:

```
{
    "title": "First Post",
    "text": "Lorem ipsum...",
    "date": "2015-01-20",
    "user_id": 45
}
{
    "title": "Second Post",
    "text": "Lorem ipsum...",
    "date": "2015-01-20",
    "user_id": 45,
    "comments": [
        {
            "name": "Anonymous",
            "text": "I love this post."
        }
    ]
}
```

Note that the first document has no comments array. As stated before, documents are schema-less, so this format is perfectly valid. The lack of a schema also means that there are no type checks at the database level. There is nothing on the database to stop an integer from being entered into the title field of a post. Schema-less data is the most powerful feature of document stores and draws many to adopt one for their apps. However, it can also be considered very dangerous, as there is one less check stopping faulty or malformed data from getting into your database.

Some document stores collect similar objects in collections of documents to make querying objects easier. However, in some document stores, all objects are queried at once. Document stores store the metadata of each object, which allows all of the values in each document to be queried and return matching documents.

The most popular document stores are **MongoDB**, **CouchDB**, and **Couchbase**.

Column family stores

Column family stores, also known as wide column stores, have many things in common with both key-value stores and document stores. Column family stores are the fastest type of NoSQL database because they are designed for large applications. Their main advantage is their ability to handle terabytes of data and still have very fast read and write speeds by distributing the data across several servers in an intelligent way.

Column family stores are also the hardest to understand, due in part to the vernacular of column family stores, as they use many of the same terms as an RDBMS, with wildly different meanings. In order to understand what a column family store is clearly, let's jump straight to an example. Let's create a simple *user to posts* association in a typical column family store.

First, we need a user table. In column family stores, data is stored and accessed via a unique key, such as a key-value store, but the contents are unstructured columns, such as a document store. Consider the following user table:

Key	Jack			John	
Column	**Full Name**	**Bio**	**Location**	**Full Name**	**Bio**
Value	Jack Stouffer	This is my about me	Michigan, USA	John Doe	This is my about me

Note that each key holds columns, which are key-value pairs as well. Also, it is not required that each key has the same number or types of columns. Each key can store hundreds of unique columns, or they can all have the same number of columns to make application development easier. This is in contrast to key-value stores, which can hold any type of data with each key. This is also slightly different to document stores, which can store types, such as arrays and dictionaries in each document. Now let's create our posts' table:

Key	Post/1			Post/2		
Column	**Title**	**Date**	**Text**	**Title**	**Date**	**Text**
Value	Hello World	2015-01-01	Post text...	Still Here	2015-02-01	Post text...

There are several things to understand about column family stores before we continue. First, in column family stores, data can only be selected via a single key or key range; there is no way to query the contents of the columns. To get around this, many programmers use an external search tool with their database, such as **Elasticsearch**, that stores the contents of columns in a searchable format and returns matching keys to be queried on the database. This limitation is why proper *schema* design is so crucial in column family stores, and must be carefully thought through before storing any data.

Second, data cannot be ordered by the content of the columns. Data can only be ordered by key, which is why the keys to the posts are integers. This allows the posts to be returned in the order in which they were entered. This was not a requirement for the user table because there is no need to sequentially order users.

Third, there are no `JOIN` operators and we cannot query for a column that would hold a user key. With our current schema, there is no way to associate a post with a user. To create this functionality, we need a third table that holds the user to post associations:

Key	Jack		
Column	Posts	Posts/1	Post/1
Value		Posts/2	Post/2

This is slightly different from the other tables we have seen so far. The `Posts` column is named a super column, which is a column that holds other columns. In this table, a super column is associated with our user key, which is holding an association of the position of a post to one post. Clever readers might ask why we wouldn't just store this association in our user table, much like how the problem would be solved in document stores. This is because regular columns and super columns cannot be held in the same table. You must choose one at the creation of each table.

To get a list of all the posts by a user, we would first have to query the post association table with our user key, use the returned list of associations to get all of the keys in the posts table, and query the post table with the keys.

If that query seems like a roundabout process to you that's because it is, and it is that way by design. The limiting nature of a column family store is what allows it to be so fast and handle so much data. Removing features such as searching by value and column name give column family stores the ability to handle hundreds of terabytes of data. It's not an exaggeration to say that SQLite is a more complex database for the programmer than a typical column family store.

For this reason, most Flask developers should steer clear of column family stores as it adds complexity to applications that isn't necessary. Unless your application is going to handle millions of reads and writes a second, using a column family store is like pounding in a nail with an atomic bomb.

The most popular column family stores are **BigTable**, **Cassandra**, and **HBase**.

Graph databases

Designed to describe and then query relationships, graph databases are like document stores but have mechanisms to create and describe links between two **nodes**.

A node in a graph store is a single piece of data, usually a collection of key-value pairs or a JSON document. Nodes can be given labels to mark them as part of a category, for example, a user or a group. After your nodes have been defined, an arbitrary number of one-way relationships between the nodes, named **links**, can be created with their own attributes. For example, if our data had two user nodes and each of the two users knew each other, we would define two "knows" links between them to describe that relationship. This would allow you to query all the people that know one user or all the people that a user knows.

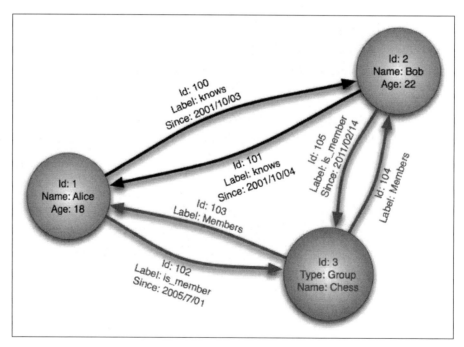

Graph stores also allow you to query by the link's attributes. This allows you to easily create otherwise complex queries, such as all of the users that one user marked as known in October 2001. Graph stores can follow links from node to node to create even more complex queries. If this example dataset had more groups, we could query for groups that people we know have joined but we haven't joined. Otherwise, we could query for people who are in the same groups as a user, but the user doesn't know them. Queries in a graph store can also follow a large number of links to answer complex questions, such as "which restaurants, that have a three-star rating or more, in New York, that serve burgers, have my friends liked?"

The most common use case for a graph database is to build a recommendation engine. For example, say we had a graph store filled with our friend data from a social networking site. Using this data, we could build a mutual friend finder by querying for users where more than two of our friends have marked them as a friend.

It is very rare for a graph database to be used as the primary data store of an application. Most uses of graph stores have each node acting as a representation of a piece of data in their main database by storing its unique identifier and a small amount of other identifying information.

The most popular graph stores are **Neo4j** and **InfoGrid**.

RDBMS versus NoSQL

NoSQL is a tool, and like any tool is has specific use cases where it excels, and use cases where some other tool would be a better fit. No one would use a screwdriver to pound in a nail. It's possible, but using a hammer would make the job easier. One large problem with NoSQL databases is that people adopt them when an RDBMS would solve the problem just as well or better.

To understand which tool to be used when, we must understand the strengths and weaknesses of both systems.

The strengths of RDBMS databases

One of the biggest strengths of an RDBMS is its maturity. The technology behind an RDBMS has existed for over 40 years and is based on the solid theory of relational algebra and relational calculus. Because of their maturity, they have a long, proven track record across many different industries of handling data in a safe and secure way.

Data safety

Safety is also one of the biggest selling points of an RDBMS. A RDBMS has several methods in place to ensure that the data entered into the database will not only be correct, but that data loss is practically nonexistent. These methods combine to form what is known as **ACID**, which stands for Atomicity, Consistency, Isolation, and Durability. ACID is a set of rules for transactions that guarantee that the transaction is handled safely.

First, atomicity requires that each transaction is all or nothing. If one part of the transaction fails, the entire transaction fails. This is much like the mentality in the Zen of Python: "Errors should never pass silently. Unless explicitly silenced." If there is a problem with the data changed or entered, the transaction should not keep operating because the proceeding operations most likely require that the previous operations were successful.

Second, consistency requires that any data the transaction modifies or adds follow the rules of each table. Such rules include type checks, user-defined constraints, such as FOREIGN KEY, cascade rules, and triggers. If any of the rules are broken, then by the atomicity rule, the transaction is thrown out.

Third, isolation requires that if the database runs transactions concurrently to speed up writes, that the outcome of the transactions would be the same if they were run serially. This is mostly a rule for database programmers and not something that web developers need to worry about.

Finally, durability requires that once a transaction is accepted, the data must never be lost, barring a hard drive failure after the transaction is accepted. If the database crashes or loses power, the durability principle requires that any data written before the problem occurred still be present when the server is backed up. This essentially means that all transactions must be written to the disk once they are accepted.

Speed and scale

A common misconception is that the ACID principle makes an RDBMS unable to scale and slow. This is only half true; it is completely possible for an RDBMS to scale. For example, an Oracle database configured by a professional database administrator can handle tens of thousands of complex queries a second. Huge companies, such as Facebook, Twitter, Tumblr, and Yahoo!, are using MySQL to great effect, and PostgreSQL is emerging as a favorite of many programmers due to its speed advantage over MySQL.

However, the largest weakness of an RDBMS is the inability to easily scale by splitting the data across several databases working in tandem. It's not impossible, as some detractors seem to imply, it's just harder than a NoSQL database. This is due to the nature of JOIN, which requires a scan of the entire data in a table, even if it is split across multiple servers. Several tools exist to help creation of a partitioned setup, but it is still mostly a job for professional database administrators.

Tools

When evaluating a programming language, the strongest points for or against adopting it are the size and activity of its community. A larger and more active community means more help if you get stuck, and more open source tools are available to use in your projects.

It's no different with databases. An RDBMS, such as MySQL or PostgreSQL, has official libraries for almost every language that is used in commercial environments and unofficial libraries for everything else. Tools, such as Excel, can easily download the latest data from one of these databases and allow the user to treat it like it was any other dataset. Several free desktop GUIs exist for each database, and some are officially supported by the databases' corporate sponsor.

The strengths of NoSQL databases

The main reason that many use NoSQL databases is its speed advantage over traditional databases. Out of the box, many NoSQL databases can outperform an RDBMS by a large amount. However, the speed comes at a cost. Many NoSQL databases, especially document stores, sacrifice consistency for availability. This means that they can handle many concurrent reads and writes, but those writes may be in conflict with one another. These databases promise "eventual consistency" rather than consistency checks on each write. In short, many NoSQL databases do not provide ACID transactions, or they are turned off by default. Once ACID checks are enabled, the speed of the database drops to near the performance of traditional databases. Every NoSQL database handles data safety differently, so it's important to read the documentation carefully before choosing one over another.

The second feature that pulls people to NoSQL is its ability to handle unformatted data. Storing data in XML or JSON allows an arbitrary structure for each document. Applications that store user-designed data have benefited greatly from the adoption of NoSQL. For example, a video game that allows players to submit their custom levels to some central repository can now store the data in a queryable format rather than in a binary blob.

The third feature that draws people to NoSQL is the ease of creating a cluster of databases working in tandem. Not having JOINs or only accessing values via keys makes splitting the data across servers a rather trivial task when compared with an RDBMS. This is due to the fact that JOINs requires a scan of the entire table, even if it is split across many different servers. JOINs become even slower when documents or keys can be assigned to a server by an algorithm as simple as the starting character of its unique identifier. For example, everything that starts with the letters A-H is sent to server one, I-P to server two, and Q-Z to server three. This makes looking up the location of data for a connected client very fast.

What database to use when

So, each database has different uses. It was stated at the beginning of the section that the main problem when programmers choose a NoSQL database for their technology stack is that they choose it when an RDBMS would work just as well. This is born out of some common misconceptions. First, people try to use a relational mindset and data model and think that they will work just as well in a NoSQL database. People usually come to this misunderstanding because the marketing on websites for NoSQL databases is misleading and encourages users to drop their current database without considering if a nonrelational model would work for their project.

Second, people believe that you must use only one data store for their application. Many applications can benefit from using more than one data store. Using a Facebook clone as an example, it could use MySQL for holding user data, redis to store session data, a document store to hold the data for the quizzes and surveys that people share with each other, and a graph database to implement a find friends feature.

If an application feature needs very fast writes, and write safety is not a primary concern, then use a document store database. If you need to store and query schema-less data, then you should use a document store database.

If an application feature needs to store something that deletes itself after a specified time, or the data does not need to be searched, then use a key-value store.

If an application feature relies on finding or describing complex relationships between two or more sets of data, then use a graph store.

If an application feature needs guaranteed write safety, each entry can fix into a specified schema, different sets of data in the database need to be compared using JOINs, or it needs constraints on the entered data, then use an RDBMS.

MongoDB in Flask

MongoDB is far and away the most popular NoSQL database. MongoDB is also the best-supported NoSQL database for Flask and Python in general. Therefore, our examples will focus on MongoDB.

MongoDB is a document store NoSQL database. Documents are stored in collections, which allow grouping of similar documents, but no similarities between documents are necessary to store a document in a collection. Documents are defined in a JSON superset named BSON, which stands for Binary JSON. BSON allows JSON to be stored in binary format rather than in string format, saving a lot of space. BSON also distinguishes between several different ways of storing numbers, such as 32-bit integers and doubles.

To understand the basics of MongoDB, we will use Flask-MongoEngine to cover the same functionality of Flask-SQLAlchemy in the previous chapters. Remember that these are just examples. There is no benefit in refactoring our current code to use MongoDB because MongoDB cannot offer any new functionality for our use case. New functionality with MongoDB will be shown in the next section.

Installing MongoDB

To install MongoDB, go to `https://www.mongodb.org/downloads` and select your OS from the tabs under the heading "Download and Run MongoDB Yourself". Every OS that has a supported version has installation instructions listed next to the download button of the installer.

To run MongoDB, go to bash and run:

```
$ mongod
```

This will run a server for as long as the window is open.

Setting Up MongoEngine

MongoEngine needs to be installed with pip before we can get started:

```
$ pip install Flask-MongoEngine
```

In the `models.py` file, a mongo object will be created that represents our database:

```
from flask.ext.mongoengine import MongoEngine

...
db = SQLAlchemy()
mongo = MongoEngine()
```

Just like the SQLAlchemy object, our mongo object needs to be initialized on the app object in __init__.py:

```
from models import db, mongo
...
db.init_app(app)
mongo.init_app(app)
```

Before our app will run, our DevConfig object in config.py needs to set up the parameters of the mongo connection:

```
MONGODB_SETTINGS = {
    'db': 'local',
    'host': 'localhost',
    'port': 27017
}
```

These are the defaults for a brand new MongoDB installation.

Defining documents

MongoEngine is an ORM based around Python's object system, specifically for MongoDB. Unfortunately, there exists no SQLAlchemy style wrapper that supports all NoSQL drivers. In an RDBMS, the implementations of SQL are so similar that creating a universal interface is possible. However, the underlying implementations of each document store are different enough that the task of creating a similar interface would be more trouble than it is worth.

Each collection in your mongo database is represented by a class that inherits from mongo.Document:

```
class Post(mongo.Document):
    title = mongo.StringField(required=True)
    text = mongo.StringField()
    publish_date = mongo.DateTimeField(
        default=datetime.datetime.now()
    )

    def __repr__(self):
        return "<Post '{}'>".format(self.title)
```

Each class variable is a representation of a key belonging to a document, which is represented in this example of a Post class. The class variable name is used as the key in the document.

Unlike SQLAlchemy, there is no need to define a primary key. A unique ID will be generated for you under the ID attribute. The preceding code would generate a BSON document that would resemble the following:

```
{
    "_id": "55366ede8b84eb00232da905",
    "title": "Post 0",
    "text": "<p>Lorem ipsum dolor...",
    "publish_date": {"$date": 1425255876037}
}
```

Field types

There are a large number of fields such that each represents a distinct category of data in Mongo. Unlike the underlying database, each field provides a type check before the document is allowed to be saved or altered. The most used fields are as follows:

- BooleanField
- DateTimeField
- DictField
- DynamicField
- EmbeddedDocumentField
- FloatField
- IntField
- ListField
- ObjectIdField
- ReferenceField
- StringField

 For a full list of fields and a detailed documentation, go to the MongoEngine website at http://docs.mongoengine.org.

The majority of these are named for the Python type they accept, and work the same as the SQLAlchemy types. However, there are some new types that have a counterpart in SQLAlchemy. `DynamicField` is a field that can hold any type of value and performs no type checks on values. `DictField` can store any Python dictionary that can be serialized by `json.dumps()`. The `ReferenceField` simply stores the unique ID of a document, and when queried, MongoEngine will return the referenced document. Counter to `ReferenceField`, `EmbeddedDocumentField` stores the passed document in the parent document, so there is no need for a second query. The `ListField` type represents a list of fields of a specific type.

This is typically used to store a list of references to other documents or a list of embedded documents to create a one-to-many relationship. If a list of unknown types is needed, `DynamicField` can be used. Each field type takes some common arguments, as shown in the following.

```
Field(
    primary_key=None
    db_field=None,
    required=False,
    default=None,
    unique=False,
    unique_with=None,
    choices=None
)
```

The `primary_key` argument specifies that you do not want MongoEngine to autogenerate a unique key, but the value of the field should be used as the ID. The value of this field will now be accessible from both the `id` attribute and the name of the field.

`db_field` defines what the key will be named in each document. If not set, it will default to the name of the class variable.

If `required` is defined as `True`, then that key must be present in the document. Otherwise, the key does not have to exist for documents of that type. When a class defined, nonexistent key is queried, it will return None.

`default` specifies the value that this field will be given if no value is defined.

If `unique` is set to `True`, MongoEngine checks to make sure that no other documents in the collection will have the same value for this field.

When passed a list of field names, `unique_with` will make sure that when taken in combination the values of all the fields will be unique for each document. This is much like multicolumn `UNIQUE` indexes in an RDBMS.

Finally, when given a list, the `choices` option limits the allowable values for that field to the elements in the list.

Types of documents

MongoEngine's method to define documents allows either flexibility or rigidity on a collection-by-collection basis. Inheriting from `mongo.Document` means that only the keys defined in the class can be saved to the database. Those keys defined in the class can be empty, but everything else will be ignored. On the other hand, if your class inherits `mongo.DynamicDocument`, any extra fields set will be treated as `DynamicFields` and will be saved with the document.

```
class Post(mongo.DynamicDocument):
    title = mongo.StringField(required=True, unique=True)
    text = mongo.StringField()
    ...
```

To show the not recommended extreme, the following class is perfectly valid; it has no required fields and allows any fields to be set:

```
class Post(mongo.DynamicDocument):
    pass
```

The last type of document is the `EmbeddedDocument`. The `EmbeddedDocument` is simply a document that is passed to an `EmbeddedDocumentField` and stored as is in the document as follows:

```
class Comment(mongo.EmbeddedDocument):
    name = mongo.StringField(required=True)
    text = mongo.StringField(required=True)
    date = mongo.DateTimeField(
        default=datetime.datetime.now()
    )
```

Why use the `EmbeddedDocumentField` over the `DictField` when they seem to perform the same function? The end result of using each is the same. However, an embedded document defines a structure for the data, while a `DictField` can be anything. for better understanding, think of it this way: `Document` is to `DynamicDocument` as `EmbeddedDocument` is to `DictField`.

The meta attribute

Using the `meta` class variable, many attributes of a document can be manually set. If you are working with an existing set of data and want to connect your classes to the collections, set the collection key of the `meta` dictionary:

```
class Post(mongo.Document):
    ...
    meta = {'collection': 'user_posts'}
```

You can also manually set the max number of documents in the collection and how large each document can be. In this example, there can be only 10,000 documents, and each document can't be larger than 2 MB:

```
class Post(mongo.Document):
    ...
    meta = {
        'collection': 'user_posts',
        'max_documents': 10000,
        'max_size': 2000000
    }
```

Indexes can also be set through MongoEngine. Indexes can be single field by using a string or multifield using a tuple:

```
class Post(mongo.Document):
    ...
    meta = {
        'collection': 'user_posts',
        'max_documents': 10000,
        'max_size': 2000000,
        'indexes': [
            'title',
            ('title', 'user')
        ]
    }
```

The default ordering of a collection can be set through the `meta` variable with the **ordering key**. When – is prepended, it tells MongoEngine to order results by descending order of that field. If + is prepended, it tells MongoEngine to order results by ascending order of that field. This default behavior is overridden if the `order_by` function is specified in a query, which will be shown in the *CRUD* section.

```
class Post(mongo.Document):
    ...
```

```
meta = {

    'collection': 'user_posts',
    'max_documents': 10000,
    'max_size': 2000000,
    'indexes': [
        'title',
        ('title', 'user')
    ],
    'ordering': ['-publish_date']

}
```

The `meta` variable can also enable user-defined documents to be inherited from, which is disabled by default. The subclass of the original document will be treated as a member of the parent class and will be stored in the same collection as follows:

```
class Post(mongo.Document):
    ...
    meta = {'allow_inheritance': True}

class Announcement(Post):
    ...
```

CRUD

As stated in *Chapter 2*, Creating Models with SQLAlchemy, there are four main forms of data manipulation that any data store must implement. They are creation of new data, reading existing data, updating existing data, and deleting data.

Create

To create a new document, just create a new instance of the class and call the `save` method.

```
>>> post = Post()
>>> post.title = "Post From The Console"
>>> post.text = "Lorem Ipsum..."
>>> post.save()
```

Otherwise, the values can be passed as keywords in the object creation:

```
>>> post = Post(title="Post From Console", text="Lorem Ipsum...")
```

Unlike SQLAlchemy, MongoEngine does not automatically save related objects stored in `ReferenceFields`. To save any changes to referenced documents along with the changes to the current document, pass `cascade` as `True`:

```
>>> post.save(cascade=True)
```

If you wish to insert a document and skip its checks against the defined parameters in the class definition, then pass validate as `False`.

```
>>> post.save(validate=False)
```

 Remember that these checks exist for a reason. Turn this off only for a very good reason

Write safety

By default, MongoDB does not wait for the data to be written to disk before acknowledging that the write occurred. This means that it is possible for writes that were acknowledged to have failed, either by hardware failure or some error when the write occurred. To ensure that the data is written to disk before Mongo confirms the write, use the `write_concern` keyword. The **write concern** tells Mongo when it should return with an acknowledgement of the write:

```
# will not wait for write and not notify client if there was an error
>>> post.save(write_concern={"w": 0})
# default behavior, will not wait for write
>>> post.save(write_concern={"w": 1})
# will wait for write
>>> post.save(write_concern={"w": 1, "j": True})
```

 As stated in the RDBMS versus NoSQL section, it's very important that you understand how the NoSQL database that you are using treats writes. To learn more about MongoDB's write concern, go to http://docs.mongodb.org/manual/reference/write-concern/.

Read

To access the documents from the database, the `objects` attribute is used. To read all of the documents in a collection, use the `all` method:

```
>>> Post.objects.all()
[<Post: "Post From The Console">]
```

To limit the number of items returned, use the `limit` method:

```
# only return five items
>>> Post.objects.limit(5).all()
```

This `limit` command is slightly different than the SQL version. In SQL, the `limit` command can also be used to skip the first results. To replicate this functionality, use the `skip` method as follows:

```
# skip the first 5 items and return items 6-10
>>> Post.objects.skip(5).limit(5).all()
```

By default, MongoDB returns the results ordered by the time of their creation. To control this, there is the `order_by` function:

```
# ascending
>>> Post.objects.order_by("+publish_date").all()
# descending
>>> Post.objects.order_by("-publish_date").all()
```

If you want only the first result from a query, use the `first` method. If your query returns nothing, and you expected it to, then use `first_or_404` to automatically abort with a 404 error. This acts exactly the same as its Flask-SQLAlchemy counterpart and is provided by Flask-MongoEngine.

```
>>> Post.objects.first()
<Post: "Post From The Console">
>>> Post.objects.first_or_404()
<Post: "Post From The Console">
```

The same behavior is available for the `get` method, which expects the query will only return one result and will raise an exception otherwise:

```
# The id value will be different your document
>>> Post.objects(id="5534451d8b84ebf422c2e4c8").get()
<Post: "Post From The Console">
>>> Post.objects(id="5534451d8b84ebf422c2e4c8").get_or_404()
<Post: "Post From The Console">
```

The `paginate` method is also present and has the exact same API as its Flask-SQLAlchemy counterpart:

```
>>> page = Post.objects.paginate(1, 10)
>>> page.items()
[<Post: "Post From The Console">]
```

Also, if your document has a `ListField` method, the `paginate_field` method on the document object can be used to paginate through the items of the list.

Filtering

If you know the exact value of the field you wish to filter by, pass its value as a keyword to the `objects` method:

```
>>> Post.objects(title="Post From The Console").first()
<Post: "Post From The Console">
```

Unlike SQLAlchemy, we cannot pass truth tests to filter our results. Instead, special keyword arguments are used to test values. For example, to find all posts published after January 1, 2015:

```
>>> Post.objects(
        publish_date__gt=datetime.datetime(2015, 1, 1)
    ).all()
[<Post: "Post From The Console">]
```

The `__gt` appended to the end of the keyword is called an operator. MongoEngine supports the following operators:

- `ne`: not equal to
- `lt`: less than
- `lte`: less than or equal to
- `gt`: greater than
- `gte`: greater than or equal to
- `not`: negate a operator, for example, `publish_date__not__gt`
- `in`: value is in list
- `nin`: value is not in list
- `mod`: *value % a == b, a* and *b* are passed as (*a, b*)
- `all`: every item in list of values provided is in the field
- `size`: the size of the list
- `exists`: value for field exists

MongoEngine also provides the following operators to test string values:

- `exact`: string equals the value

- iexact: string equals the value (case insensitive)
- contains: string contains the value
- icontains: string contains the value (case insensitive)
- startswith: string starts with the value
- istartswith: string starts with the value (case insensitive)
- endswith: string ends with the value
- iendswith: string ends with the value (case insensitive) Update

These operators can be combined to create the same powerful queries that were created in the previous sections. For example, to find all of the posts that were created after January 1, 2015 that don't have the word post in the title, the body text starts with the word Lorem, and ordered by the publish date with the latest one:

```
>>> Post.objects(
    title__not__icontains="post",
    text__istartswith="Lorem",
    publish_date__gt=datetime.datetime(2015, 1, 1),
).order_by("-publish_date").all()
```

However, if there is some complex query that cannot be represented by these tools, then a raw Mongo query can be passed as well:

```
>>> Post.objects(__raw__={"title": "Post From The Console"})
```

Update

To update objects, the update method is called on the results of a query.

```
>>> Post.objects(
        id="5534451d8b84ebf422c2e4c8"
    ).update(text="Ipsum lorem")
```

If your query should only return one value, then use update_one to only modify the first result:

```
>>> Post.objects(
        id="5534451d8b84ebf422c2e4c8"
    ).update_one(text="Ipsum lorem")
```

Unlike traditional SQL, there are many different ways to change a value in MongoDB. Operators are used to change the values of a field in different ways:

- `set`: This sets a value (same as given earlier)
- `unset`: This deletes a value and removes the key
- `inc`: This increments a value
- `dec`: This decrements a value
- `push`: This appends a value to a list
- `push_all`: This appends several values to a list
- `pop`: This removes the first or last element of a list
- `pull`: This removes a value from a list
- `pull_all`: This removes several values from a list
- `add_to_set`: This adds value to a list only if its not in the list already

For example, if a `Python` value needs to be added to a `ListField` named tags for all `Post` documents that have the `MongoEngine` tag:

```
>>> Post.objects(
        tags__in="MongoEngine",
        tags__not__in="Python"
    ).update(push__tags="Python")
```

The same write concern parameters to save exist for updates.

```
>>> Post.objects(
        tags__in="MongoEngine"
    ).update(push__tags="Python", write_concern={"w": 1, "j": True})
```

Delete

To delete a document instance, call its `delete` method:

```
>>> post = Post.objects(
        id="5534451d8b84ebf422c2e4c8"
    ).first()
>>> post.delete()
```

Relationships in NoSQL

As we created relationships in SQLAlchemy, we can create relationships between objects in MongoEngine. Only with MongoEngine, we will be doing so without JOIN operators.

One-to-many relationships

There are two ways to create a one-to-many relationship in MongoEngine. The first method is to create a relationship between two documents by using a ReferenceField to point to the ID of another object.

```
class Post(mongo.Document):
    ...
    user = mongo.ReferenceField(User)
```

Accessing the property of the ReferenceField gives direct access to the referenced object as follows:

```
>>> user = User.objects.first()
>>> post = Post.objects.first()
>>> post.user = user
>>> post.save()
>>> post.user
<User Jack>
```

Unlike SQLAlchemy, MongoEngine has no way to access objects that have relationships to another object. With SQLAlchemy, a db.relationship variable could be declared, which allows a user object to access all of the posts with a matching user_id column. No such parallel exists in MongoEngine.

A solution is to get the user ID for the posts you wish to search for and filter with the user field. This is the same thing as SQLAlchemy did behind the scenes, but we are just doing it manually:

```
>>> user = User.objects.first()
>>> Post.objects(user__id=user.id)
```

The second way to create a one-to-many relationship is to use an EmbeddedDocumentField with an EmbeddedDocument:

```
class Post(mongo.Document):
    title = mongo.StringField(required=True)
    text = mongo.StringField()
```

```
publish_date = mongo.DateTimeField(
    default=datetime.datetime.now()
)
user = mongo.ReferenceField(User)
comments = mongo.ListField(
    mongo.EmbeddedDocumentField(Comment)
)
```

Accessing the `comments` property gives a list of all the embedded documents. To add a new comment to the post, treat it like a list and append `comment` documents to it:

```
>>> comment = Comment()
>>> comment.name = "Jack"
>>> comment.text = "I really like this post!"
>>> post.comments.append(comment)
>>> post.save()
>>> post.comments
[<Comment 'I really like this post!'>]
```

Note that there was no call to a `save` method on the comment variable. This is because the comment document is not a real document, it is only an abstraction of the `DictField`. Also, keep in mind that documents can only be 16 MB large, so be careful how many `EmbeddedDocumentFields` are on each document and how many `EmbeddedDocuments` each one is holding.

Many-to-many relationships

The concept of a many-to-many relationship does not exist in document store databases. This is because with `ListFields` they become completely irrelevant. To idiomatically create the tag feature for the `Post` object, add a list of strings:

```
class Post(mongo.Document):
    title = mongo.StringField(required=True)
    text = mongo.StringField()
    publish_date = mongo.DateTimeField(
        default=datetime.datetime.now()
    )
    user = mongo.ReferenceField(User)
    comments = mongo.ListField(
        mongo.EmbeddedDocumentField(Comment)
    )
    tags = mongo.ListField(mongo.StringField())
```

Now when we wish to query for all of the `Post` objects that have a specific tag, or many tags, it is a simple query:

```
>>> Post.objects(tags__in="Python").all()
>>> Post.objects(tags__all=["Python", "MongoEngine"]).all()
```

For the list of roles on each user object, the optional choices argument can be given to restrict the possible roles:

```
available_roles = ('admin', 'poster', 'default')

class User(mongo.Document):
    username = mongo.StringField(required=True)
    password = mongo.StringField(required=True)
    roles = mongo.ListField(
        mongo.StringField(choices=available_roles)
    )

    def __repr__(self):
        return '<User {}>'.format(self.username)
```

Leveraging the power of NoSQL

So far, our MongoEngine code should look like the following:

```
available_roles = ('admin', 'poster', 'default')

class User(mongo.Document):
    username = mongo.StringField(required=True)
    password = mongo.StringField(required=True)
    roles = mongo.ListField(
        mongo.StringField(choices=available_roles)
    )

    def __repr__(self):
        return '<User {}>'.format(self.username)


class Comment(mongo.EmbeddedDocument):
    name = mongo.StringField(required=True)
    text = mongo.StringField(required=True)
    date = mongo.DateTimeField(
```

```
            default=datetime.datetime.now()
        )

    def __repr__(self):
        return "<Comment '{}'>".format(self.text[:15])


class Post(mongo.Document):
    title = mongo.StringField(required=True)
    text = mongo.StringField()
    publish_date = mongo.DateTimeField(
        default=datetime.datetime.now()
    )
    user = mongo.ReferenceField(User)
    comments = mongo.ListField(
        mongo.EmbeddedDocumentField(Comment)
    )
    tags = mongo.ListField(mongo.StringField())

    def __repr__(self):
        return "<Post '{}'>".format(self.title)
```

This code implements the same functionality as the SQLAlchemy models. To show the unique power of NoSQL, let's add a feature that would be possible with SQLAlchemy, but that is much more difficult: different post types, each with their own custom bodies. This will be much like the functionality of the popular blog platform, Tumblr.

To begin, allow your post type to act as a parent class and remove the text field from the Post class as not all posts will have text on them:

```
class Post(mongo.Document):
    title = mongo.StringField(required=True)
    publish_date = mongo.DateTimeField(
        default=datetime.datetime.now()
    )
    user = mongo.ReferenceField(Userm)
    comments = mongo.ListField(
        mongo.EmbeddedDocumentField(Commentm)
    )
    tags = mongo.ListField(mongo.StringField())

    meta = {
        'allow_inheritance': True
    }
```

Each post type will inherit from the Post class. Doing so will allow the code to treat any Post subclass as if it were a Post. Our blogging app will have four types of posts: a normal blog post, an image post, a video post, and a quote post.

```python
class BlogPost(Post):
    text = db.StringField(required=True)

    @property
    def type(self):
        return "blog"

class VideoPost(Post):
    url = db.StringField(required=True)

    @property
    def type(self):
        return "video"

class ImagePost(Post):
    image_url = db.StringField(required=True)

    @property
    def type(self):
        return "image"

class QuotePost(Post):
    quote = db.StringField(required=True)
    author = db.StringField(required=True)

    @property
    def type(self):
        return "quote"
```

Our post creation page needs to be able to create each of these post types. The PostForm object in forms.py, which handles post creation, will need to be modified to handle the new fields first. We will add a selection field that determines the type of post, an author field for the quote type, an image field to hold a URL, and a video field that will hold the embedded HTML iframe. The quote and blog post content will both share the text field as follows:

```python
class PostForm(Form):
    title = StringField('Title', [
        DataRequired(),
        Length(max=255)
    ])
```

```
type = SelectField('Post Type', choices=[
    ('blog', 'Blog Post'),
    ('image', 'Image'),
    ('video', 'Video'),
    ('quote', 'Quote')
])
text = TextAreaField('Content')
image = StringField('Image URL', [URL(), Length(max=255)])
video = StringField('Video Code', [Length(max=255)])
author = StringField('Author', [Length(max=255)])
```

The `new_post` view function in the `blog.py` controller will also need to be updated to handle the new post types:

```
@blog_blueprint.route('/new', methods=['GET', 'POST'])
@login_required
@poster_permission.require(http_exception=403)
def new_post():
    form = PostForm()

    if form.validate_on_submit():
        if form.type.data == "blog":
            new_post = BlogPost()
            new_post.text = form.text.data
        elif form.type.data == "image":
            new_post = ImagePost()
            new_post.image_url = form.image.data
        elif form.type.data == "video":
            new_post = VideoPost()
            new_post.video_object = form.video.data
        elif form.type.data == "quote":
            new_post = QuotePost()
            new_post.text = form.text.data
            new_post.author = form.author.data

        new_post.title = form.title.data
        new_post.user = User.objects(
            username=current_user.username
        ).one()

        new_post.save()

    return render_template('new.html', form=form)
```

The `new.html` file that renders our form object will need to display the new fields added to the form:

```
<form method="POST" action="{{ url_for('.new_post') }}">
...
<div class="form-group">
    {{ form.type.label }}
    {% if form.type.errors %}
        {% for e in form.type.errors %}
            <p class="help-block">{{ e }}</p>
        {% endfor %}
    {% endif %}
    {{ form.type(class_='form-control') }}
</div>
...
<div id="image_group" class="form-group">
    {{ form.image.label }}
    {% if form.image.errors %}
        {% for e in form.image.errors %}
            <p class="help-block">{{ e }}</p>
        {% endfor %}
    {% endif %}
    {{ form.image(class_='form-control') }}
</div>
<div id="video_group" class="form-group">
    {{ form.video.label }}
    {% if form.video.errors %}
        {% for e in form.video.errors %}
            <p class="help-block">{{ e }}</p>
        {% endfor %}
    {% endif %}
    {{ form.video(class_='form-control') }}
</div>
<div id="author_group" class="form-group">
    {{ form.author.label }}
        {% if form.author.errors %}
            {% for e in form.author.errors %}
                <p class="help-block">{{ e }}</p>
            {% endfor %}
        {% endif %}
        {{ form.author(class_='form-control') }}
</div>
<input class="btn btn-primary" type="submit" value="Submit">
</form>
```

Now that we have our new inputs, we can add in some JavaScript to show and hide the fields based on the type of post:

```
{% block js %}
<script src="//cdn.ckeditor.com/4.4.7/standard/ckeditor.js"></script>
<script>
    CKEDITOR.replace('editor');

    $(function () {
        $("#image_group").hide();
        $("#video_group").hide();
        $("#author_group").hide();

        $("#type").on("change", function () {
            switch ($(this).val()) {
                case "blog":
                    $("#text_group").show();
                    $("#image_group").hide();
                    $("#video_group").hide();
                    $("#author_group").hide();
                    break;
                case "image":
                    $("#text_group").hide();
                    $("#image_group").show();
                    $("#video_group").hide();
                    $("#author_group").hide();
                    break;
                case "video":
                    $("#text_group").hide();
                    $("#image_group").hide();
                    $("#video_group").show();
                    $("#author_group").hide();
                    break;
                case "quote":
                    $("#text_group").show();
                    $("#image_group").hide();
                    $("#video_group").hide();
                    $("#author_group").show();
                    break;
            }
```

```
        });
    })
</script>
{% endblock %}
```

Finally, the `post.html` needs to be able to display our post types correctly. We have the following:

```html
<div class="col-lg-12">
    {{ post.text | safe }}
</div>
All that is needed is to replace this with:
<div class="col-lg-12">
    {% if post.type == "blog" %}
        {{ post.text | safe }}
    {% elif post.type == "image" %}
        <img src="{{ post.image_url }}" alt="{{ post.title }}">
    {% elif post.type == "video" %}
        {{ post.video_object | safe }}
    {% elif post.type == "quote" %}
        <blockquote>
            {{ post.text | safe }}
        </blockquote>
        <p>{{ post.author }}</p>
    {% endif %}
</div>
```

Summary

In this chapter, the fundamental differences between NoSQL and traditional SQL systems were laid out. We explored the main types of NoSQL systems and why an application might need, or not need, to be designed with a NoSQL database. Using our app's models as a base, the power of MongoDB and MongoEngine was shown by how simple it was to set up complex relationships and inheritance. In the next chapter, our blogging application will be extended with a feature designed for other programmers who wish to use our site to build their own service, that is, RESTful endpoints.

8
Building RESTful APIs

Representational State Transfer, or **REST**, is a method of transferring information between a client and a server. On the Web, REST is used on top of HTTP and allows browsers and servers to easily communicate by leveraging basic HTTP commands. By using HTTP commands, REST is platform and programming language agnostic, and decouples the client and the server for easier development. This is typically used in JavaScript applications that need to pull or update user information on the server. REST is also used to provide outside developers with a common interface to user data. For example, Facebook and Twitter use REST in their application program interface (**API**), to allow developers to get information without having to parse the website's HTML.

What is REST

Before getting into the details of REST, let's look at an example. With a client, in this case, a web browser, and a server, the client sends a request to the server over HTTP for some models as follows:

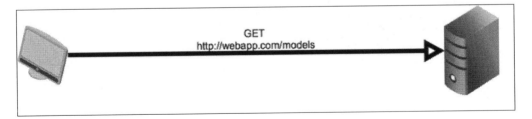

The server will then respond with a document containing all the models.

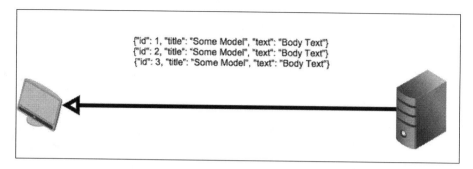

The client can then modify the data on the server through a PUT HTTP request:

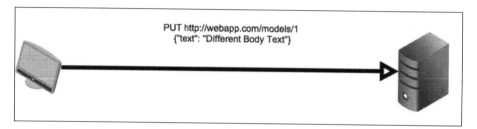

Then the server will respond that it has modified the data. This is a very simplified example, but it will serve as a backdrop to how REST is defined.

Rather than a strict standard, REST lays out a set of constraints on communications to define a methodology that can be implemented in many ways. These constraints are born out of years of trial and error with other communication protocols, such as **Remote Procedure Call (RPC)** or **Simple Object Access Protocol (SOAP)**. These protocols fell by the wayside due to their strictness, verboseness, and the difficulty in creating APIs with them. The issues with these systems were identified, and REST's constraints were created to keep these issues from happening again.

The first constraint requires that the client and the server must have a separation of concerns. The client cannot handle permanent data storage, and the server cannot handle anything with the user interface.

The second constraint is that the server must be stateless. What this means is that any information that is necessary to handle requests is stored in the request itself or by the client. An example of the server being stateless is the session object in Flask. The session object does not store its information on the server, but stores it on the client in a cookie. The cookie is sent along with every request for the server to parse and determine if the necessary data for the requested resource is stored inside it rather than the server storing session information for every user.

The third constraint is that all resources provided must have a uniform interface. There are many different parts to this constraint, which are as follows:

- The interface is based around resources, which are models in our case.

- Data sent by the server is not the actual data in the server, but a representation. For example, the actual database is not sent with each request, but a JSON abstraction of the data.

- The data sent by the server is enough to allow the client to modify the data on the server. In the preceding example, the IDs passed to the client filled this role.

- Every resource provided by the API must be represented and accessed in the same manner. For example, one resource cannot be represented in XML and one in JSON, one over raw TCP and one over HTTP.

The final constraint is that the system must allow for layers. Load balancers, proxies, caches, and other servers and services can act between the client and the server as long as the final result is the same as if they were not there.

When a system adheres to all these constraints, it is considered to be a RESTful system. The most common forms of RESTful systems are built of HTTP and JSON. Each resource is located on its own URL path and modified with different HTTP request types. Generally, it takes the following form:

HTTP method	URL	Action
GET	`http://host/resource`	Get all the resource representations
GET	`http://host/resource/1`	Get the resource with an ID of one
POST	`http://host/resource`	Create a new resource from the form data in the POST
PUT	`http://host/resource/1`	Modify the existing data of the resource with the ID of one
DELETE	`http://host/resource/1`	Delete the resource with the ID of one

As an example, a response to the second GET request would look like the following:

```
{
    "id": 100,
    "date": "2015-03-02T00:24:36+00:00",
    "title": "Resource #98"
}
```

In REST APIs, it is also very important to return the correct HTTP status code with the response data, to notify the clients of what actually happened on the server without the client resorting to parsing the returned message. Here is the list of the main HTTP codes used in REST APIs and their meaning.

HTTP code	Name	Meaning
200	OK	The default code of HTTP. The request was successful, and the data was returned.
201	Created	The request was successful, and a new resource was created on the server.
204	No content	The request was successful, but the response returned no content.
400	Bad request	The request was denied because of some perceived client error—either a malformed request or missing required data.
401	Unauthorized	The request was denied because the client is not authenticated and should authenticate before requesting this resource again.
403	Forbidden	The request was denied because the client does not have permission to access this resource. This is in contrast to the 401 code, which assumes that the user is not authenticated. The 403 code says the resource is not accessible regardless of authentication.
404	Not found	The requested resource does not exist.
405	Method not allowed	The request was denied because the HTTP method is not available for the URL.

Setting up a RESTful Flask API

In our app, we will create a RESTful interface to the blog post data in our database. The representations of the data will be sent as JSON. The data will be retrieved and modified using the general form in the preceding table, but the URI will be /api/posts.

We could just use the standard Flask views to create the API, but the Flask extension **Flask Restful** makes the task much easier.

To install Flask Restful:

```
$ pip install Flask-Restful
```

In the `extensions.py` file, initialize the `Api` object that will handle all the routes:

```
from flask.ext.restful import Api
...
rest_api = Api()
```

The control logic and views for our Post API should be stored in a new folder named `rest` in the `controllers` folder. In this folder, we will need an empty `__init__.py` and a file named `post.py`. Inside `post.py`, let's create a simple *Hello World* example:

```
from flask.ext.restful import Resource


class PostApi(Resource):
    def get(self):
        return {'hello': 'world'}
```

In Flask Restful, every REST resource is defined as a class that inherits from the `Resource` object. Much like the `MethodView` object shown in *Chapter 4, Creating Controllers with Blueprints*, any class that inherits from the `Resource` object defines its logic with methods named after the HTTP methods. For example, when the `GET` HTTP method hits the `PostApi` class, the `get` method will be executed.

Just like the other Flask extensions we used, the `Api` object will need to be initialized on the app object in the `__init__.py` file, which holds the `create_app` function. The `PostApi` class will also have its route defined with the `add_resource()` method of the `Api` object:

```
from .extensions import (
    bcrypt,
    oid,
    login_manager,
    principals,
    rest_api
)
from .controllers.rest.post import PostApi


def create_app(object_name):
    ...
    rest_api.add_resource(PostApi, '/api/post')
    rest_api.init_app(app)
```

Now, if you open the `/api/post` URI in the browser, the *Hello World* JSON will be displayed.

GET requests

For some of our GET, PUT, and DELETE requests, our API will need the ID of the
Post to modify. The add_resource method can take multiple routes, so let's add
the second route that captures the passed ID:

```
rest_api.add_resource(
    PostApi,
    '/api/post',
    '/api/post/<int:post_id>',
    endpoint='api'
)
```

Now the get method will need to accept post_id as a keyword argument:

```
class PostApi(Resource):
    def get(self, post_id=None):
        if post_id:
            return {"id": post_id}

        return {"hello": "world"}
```

The data to be sent to the client must be a representation of the Post objects in
JSON, so how will our Post objects be translated? Flask Restful provides a way of
translating any object to JSON through the fields object and the marshal_with
function decorator.

Output formatting

The output format is defined by creating a dictionary of field objects that represent
basic types. The key of the field defines what attribute the field will try to translate.
By passing the dictionary to the marshal_with decorator, any object the get method
attempts to return will be first translated with the dictionary. This also works for lists
of objects:

```
from flask import abort
from flask.ext.restful import Resource, fields, marshal_with
from webapp.models import Post

post_fields = {
    'title': fields.String(),
    'text': fields.String(),
    'publish_date': fields.DateTime(dt_format='iso8601')
```

```
}

class PostApi(Resource):
    @marshal_with(post_fields)
    def get(self, post_id=None):
        if post_id:
            post = Post.query.get(post_id)
            if not post:
                abort(404)

            return post
        else:
            posts = Post.query.all()
            return posts
```

While reloading the API in the browser, every Post object will be shown in JSON format. However, the problem is that the API should not return the HTML from the WYSIWYG editor in the post creation form. As stated earlier, the server should not be concerned with UI, and HTML is purely for output specification. To solve this, we will need a custom field object that strips HTML from strings. In a new file in the rest folder named fields.py, add the following:

```
from HTMLParser import HTMLParser
from flask.ext.restful import fields

class HTMLStripper(HTMLParser):
    def __init__(self):
        self.reset()
        self.fed = []

    def handle_data(self, d):
        self.fed.append(d)

    def get_data(self):
        return ''.join(self.fed)

    def strip_tags(html):
        s = HTMLStripper()
        s.feed(html)

        return s.get_data()

class HTMLField(fields.Raw):
    def format(self, value):
        return strip_tags(str(value))
```

Now, our `post_fields` dictionary should be updated to work with the new field:

```
from .fields import HTMLField

post_fields = {
    'title': fields.String(),
    'text': HTMLField(),
    'publish_date': fields.DateTime(dt_format='iso8601')
}
```

Using the standard library `HTMLParser` module, we now have a `strip_tags` function that will return any string cleaned of HTML tags. A new field type `HTMLfield` is defined by inheriting from the `fields.Raw` class and sending values through the `strip_tags` function. If the page is reloaded once again, all the HTML is gone and just the text remains.

Flask Restful provides many default fields:

- `fields.String`: This converts the value using `str()`.
- `fields.FormattedString`: This passes formatted string in Python with the variable name in brackets.
- `fields.Url`: This provides the same functionality as the Flask `url_for` function.
- `fields.DateTime`: This converts a Python `date` or `datetime` object to a string. The format keyword argument specifies if the string should be an `ISO8601` date or an `RFC822` date.
- `fields.Float`: This converts the value to a string representation of a float.
- `fields.Integer`: This converts the value to a string representation of an integer.
- `fields.Nested`: This allows nested objects to be represented by another dictionary of field objects.
- `fields.List`: Much like the MongoEngine API, this field takes another field type as an argument and tries to convert a list of values into a JSON list of the field types.
- `fields.Boolean`: This converts the value to a string representation of a boolean argument.

There are two more fields that should be added to the returned data: the author and the tags. The comments will be left out because they should be contained under their own resource.

```
nested_tag_fields = {
```

```
    'id': fields.Integer(),
    'title': fields.String()
}

post_fields = {
    'author': fields.String(attribute=lambda x: x.user.username),
    'title': fields.String(),
    'text': HTMLField(),
    'tags': fields.List(fields.Nested(nested_tag_fields)),
    'publish_date': fields.DateTime(dt_format='iso8601')
}
```

The `author` field uses the attribute keyword argument of the `field` class. This allows any attribute of the object to be represented rather than just base-level properties. Because the many-to-many relationship of the tags returns a list of objects, the same solution cannot be used with the tags. Using the `NestedField` type inside a `ListField` and another dictionary of fields, a list of tag dictionaries can now be returned. This has the added benefit for the end users of the API of giving them a tag ID to easily query as if there was a tag API.

Request arguments

While sending a GET request to the base of the resource, our API currently sends all the Post objects in the database. This is acceptable if the number of objects is low or the number of people using the API is low. However, if either increases, the API will put a large amount of stress on the database. Much like the Web interface, the API should be paginated as well.

In order to achieve this, our API will need to accept a GET query string parameter `page` that specifies which page to load. Flask Restful provides a method to grab request data and parse it. If the required arguments aren't there, or the types don't match, Flask Restful will autocreate a JSON error message. In a new file in the rest folder named `parsers.py`, add the following code:

```
from flask.ext.restful import reqparse

post_get_parser = reqparse.RequestParser()
post_get_parser.add_argument(
    'page',
    type=int,
    location=['args', 'headers'],
    required=False
)
```

Now the `PostApi` class will need to be updated to work with our parser:

```
from .parsers import post_get_parser


class PostApi(Resource):
    @marshal_with(post_fields)
    def get(self, post_id=None):
        if post_id:
            post = Post.query.get(post_id)
            if not post:
                abort(404)

            return post
        else:
            args = post_get_parser.parse_args()
            page = args['page'] or 1
            posts = Post.query.order_by(
                Post.publish_date.desc()
            ).paginate(page, 30)

            return posts.items
```

In the preceding example, the `RequestParser` looks for the `page` variable in either the query string or the request header and returns the page of Post objects from that page.

After a parser object is created with `RequestParser`, arguments can be added using the `add_argument` method. The first argument of `add_argument` is the key of the argument to parse, but `add_argument` also takes a lot of keyword arguments:

- `action`: This is what the parser does with the value after it has been successfully parsed. The two available options are `store` and `append`. `store` adds the parsed value to the returned dictionary. `append` adds the parsed value to the end of a list in the dictionary.

- `case_sensitive`: This is a `boolean` argument to allow or disallow the keys to be case insensitive.

- `choices`: This is like MongoEngine, a list of the allowed values for the argument.

- `default`: This is the value produced if the argument is absent from the request.

- `dest`: This is the key to add the parsed value in the return data.

- `help`: This is a message to return to the user if validation fails.
- `ignore`: This is a `boolean` argument to allow or disallow failures of the type conversion.
- `location`: this indicates where to look for the data. The locations available are:
  - `args` to look in the GET query string
  - `headers` to look in the HTTP request headers
  - `form` to look in the HTTP POST data
  - `cookies` to look in the HTTP cookies
  - `json` to look in any sent JSON
  - `files` to look in the POST file data
- `required`: this is a `boolean` argument to determine if the argument is optional.
- `store_missing`: this is a `boolean` argument to determine if the default value should be stored if the argument is not in the request.
- `type`: this is the Python type to convert the passed value.

Using the Flask Restful parser, it is very easy to add new parameters to the API. For example, let's add a user argument that allows us to search for all posts by a user. First, in the `parsers.py` file, add the following:

```python
post_get_parser = reqparse.RequestParser()
post_get_parser.add_argument(
    'page',
    type=int,
    location=['json', 'args', 'headers']
)
post_get_parser.add_argument(
    'user',
    type=str,
    location=['json', 'args', 'headers']
)
```

Then, in `post.py`, add the following:

```python
class PostApi(Resource):
    @marshal_with(post_fields)
    def get(self, post_id=None):
        if post_id:
            post = Post.query.get(post_id)
            if not post:
```

```
                    abort(404)

                return post
        else:
            args = post_get_parser.parse_args()
            page = args['page'] or 1

            if args['user']:
                user = User.query.filter_by(
                    username=args['user']
                ).first()
                if not user:
                    abort(404)

                posts = user.posts.order_by(
                    Post.publish_date.desc()
                ).paginate(page, 30)
            else:
                posts = Post.query.order_by(
                    Post.publish_date.desc()
                ).paginate(page, 30)

        return posts.items
```

When the Flask `abort` function is called from a `Resource`, Flask Restful will automatically create an error message to be returned with the status code.

POST requests

Using our new knowledge of the Flask Restful parser, the POST endpoint can be added. First, we will need a parser that will take a title, the body text, and a list of tags. In the `parser.py` file, add the following:

```
post_post_parser = reqparse.RequestParser()
post_post_parser.add_argument(
    'title',
    type=str,
    required=True,
    help="Title is required"
)
post_post_parser.add_argument(
    'text',
```

```
        type=str,
        required=True,
        help="Body text is required"
    )
post_post_parser.add_argument(
        'tags',
        type=str,
        action='append'
    )
```

Next, the `PostApi` class will need a `post` method to handle incoming requests. The `post` method will use the given values for the title and body text. Also, if the tags key exists, then add the tags to the post, which creates new tags if the passed ones do not exist:

```
import datetime
from .parsers import (
    post_get_parser,
    post_post_parser
)
from webapp.models import db, User, Post, Tag


class PostApi(Resource):
    ...
    def post(self, post_id=None):
        if post_id:
            abort(400)
        else:
            args = post_post_parser.parse_args(strict=True)
            new_post = Post(args['title'])
            new_post.date = datetime.datetime.now()
            new_post.text = args['text']

            if args['tags']:
                for item in args['tags']:
                    tag = Tag.query.filter_by(title=item).first()

                    # Add the tag if it exists.
                    # If not, make a new tag
                    if tag:
                        new_post.tags.append(tag)
                    else:
```

```
                    new_tag = Tag(item)
                    new_post.tags.append(new_tag)

            db.session.add(new_post)
            db.session.commit()
            return new_post.id, 201
```

At the `return` statement, if a tuple is returned, the second argument is treated as the status code. There is also a third value that acts as extra header values by passing a dictionary.

In order to test this code, a different tool than the web browser has to be used, as creating custom POST requests without a browser plugin is very difficult in a browser. A tool named curl will be used instead. **Curl** is a command-line tool included in Bash that allows for creation and manipulation of HTTP requests. To perform a GET request with curl, just pass the URL:

```
$ curl http://localhost:5000/api/post/1
```

To pass POST variables, the d flag is used:

```
$ curl -d "title=From REST" \
-d "text=The body text from REST" \
-d "tag=Python" \
http://localhost:5000/api/post
```

The id of the newly created post should be returned. However, if you now load the post you created in the browser, an error should appear. This is because our Post object had no user associated with it. In order to have Post objects assigned to users and for only authenticated users of the website to have permission to POST posts, we need to create an authentication system.

Authentication

To solve our authentication problems, Flask-Login could be used and the cookie data from the login could be checked. However, this would require developers who wish to use our API to have their program login through the web interface. We could also have developers send their login data with every request, but it's a good design practice to only send sensitive information when absolutely necessary. Instead, our API will provide an `auth` endpoint that allows them to send login credentials and get an access token back.

This `access` token will be created by the Python library *it's dangerous*, which Flask uses to encode the session data on a cookie, so it should already be installed. The token will be a Python dictionary cryptographically signed by the app's secret key containing the id of the user. This token has an expiration date encoded inside it that will not allow it to be used after it expires. This means that even if the token is stolen by a malicious user, it will only be useful for a limited amount of time before the client has to reauthenticate. First, a new parser is needed to handle parsing the username and password data:

```
user_post_parser = reqparse.RequestParser()
user_post_parser.add_argument('username', type=str, required=True)
user_post_parser.add_argument('password', type=str, required=True)
```

In a new file named `auth.py` inside the `rest` folder, add the following code:

```
from flask import abort, current_app

from .parsers import user_post_parser
from itsdangerous import TimedJSONWebSignatureSerializer as Serializer

class AuthApi(Resource):
    def post(self):
        args = user_post_parser.parse_args()
        user = User.query.filter_by(
            username=args['username']
        ).one()

        if user.check_password(args['password']):
            s = Serializer(
                current_app.config['SECRET_KEY'],
                expires_in=600
            )
            return {"token": s.dumps({'id': user.id})}
        else:
            abort(401)
```

Do not allow users to send their login credentials across an unsecured connection! HTTPS is required if you wish to protect your user's data. The best solution would be to require HTTPS for your entire app to avoid the possibility.

Users of our API will have to pass the token received from this resource to any method that requires user credentials. However, first we need a function that verifies the token. In the `models.py` file, the `verify_auth_token` will be a `staticmethod` on the `User` object:

```python
from itsdangerous import (
    TimedJSONWebSignatureSerializer as Serializer,
    BadSignature,
    SignatureExpired
)
from flask import current_app

class User(db.Model):
...

    @staticmethod
    def verify_auth_token(token):
        s = Serializer(current_app.config['SECRET_KEY'])

        try:
            data = s.loads(token)
        except SignatureExpired:
            return None
        except BadSignature:
            return None

        user = User.query.get(data['id'])
        return user
```

Our POST parser needs a token argument to accept the `auth` token:

```python
post_post_parser = reqparse.RequestParser()
post_post_parser.add_argument(
    'token',
    type=str,
    required=True,
    help="Auth Token is required to create posts"
)
```

Now, our `post` method can properly add new posts as follows:

```python
class PostApi(Resource):
    def get(self, post_id=None):
        ...

    def post(self, post_id=None):
        if post_id:
```

```
        abort(405)
    else:
        args = post_post_parser.parse_args(strict=True)

        user = User.verify_auth_token(args['token'])
        if not user:
            abort(401)

        new_post = Post(args['title'])
        new_post.user = user
        ...
```

Using curl, our `auth` and `post` APIs can now be tested. For the sake of brevity, the token is omitted here as it is very long:

```
$ curl -d "username=user" \
-d "password=password" \
http://localhost:5000/api/auth


{token: <the token>}


$ curl -d "title=From REST" \
-d "text=this is from REST" \
-d "token=<the token>" \
-d "tags=Python" \
-d "tags=Flask" \
http://localhost:5000/api/post
```

PUT requests

As listed in the table at the beginning of this chapter, PUT requests are for changing the values of existing resources. Like the `post` method, the first thing to be done is to create a new parser in `parsers.py`:

```
post_put_parser = reqparse.RequestParser()
post_put_parser.add_argument(
    'token',
    type=str,
    required=True,
    help="Auth Token is required to edit posts"
)
post_put_parser.add_argument(
```

```
    'title',
    type=str
)
post_put_parser.add_argument(
    'text',
    type=str
)
post_put_parser.add_argument(
    'tags',
    type=str,
    action='append'
)
```

The logic for the `put` method is very similar to the `post` method. The main difference is that each change is optional and any request that does not provide a `post_id` is denied:

```
from .parsers import (
    post_get_parser,
    post_post_parser,
    post_put_parser
)


class PostApi(Resource):
    @marshal_with(post_fields)
    def get(self, post_id=None):
        ...

    def post(self, post_id=None):
        ...

    def put(self, post_id=None):
        if not post_id:
            abort(400)

        post = Post.query.get(post_id)
        if not post:
            abort(404)

        args = post_put_parser.parse_args(strict=True)
        user = User.verify_auth_token(args['token'])
        if not user:
```

```
        abort(401)
    if user != post.user:
        abort(403)

    if args['title']:
        post.title = args['title']

    if args['text']:
        post.text = args['text']

    if args['tags']:
        for item in args['tags']:
            tag = Tag.query.filter_by(title=item).first()

            # Add the tag if it exists. If not, make a new tag
            if tag:
                post.tags.append(tag)
            else:
                new_tag = Tag(item)
                post.tags.append(new_tag)

    db.session.add(post)
    db.session.commit()
    return post.id, 201
```

To test this method, curl can also create PUT requests with the -x flag:

```
$ curl -X PUT \
-d "title=Modified From REST" \
-d "text=this is from REST" \
-d "token=<the token>" \
-d "tags=Python" -d "tags=Flask" -d "tags=REST" \
http://localhost:5000/api/post/101
```

DELETE requests

Finally, we have the DELETE request, which is the simplest of the four supported methods. The main difference with the delete method is that it returns no content, which is the accepted standard with DELETE requests:

```
class PostApi(Resource):
    @marshal_with(post_fields)
```

```
def get(self, post_id=None):
    ...


def post(self, post_id=None):
    ...


def put(self, post_id=None):
    ...


def delete(self, post_id=None):
    if not post_id:
        abort(400)

    post = Post.query.get(post_id)
    if not post:
        abort(404)

    args = post_delete_parser.parse_args(strict=True)
    user = verify_auth_token(args['token'])
    if user != post.user:
        abort(403)

    db.session.delete(post)
    db.session.commit()
    return "", 204
```

Again, we can test with:

```
$ curl -X DELETE\
-d "token=<the token>"\
http://localhost:5000/api/post/102
```

If everything is successfully deleted, you should receive a 204 status code and nothing should show up.

Before we move on from REST completely, there is one final challenge to the reader to test your understanding of Flask Restful. Try to create a comments API that is not only modifiable from `http://localhost:5000/api/comments`, but also allow developers to modify only those comments on a specific post by using the URL `http://localhost:5000/api/post/<int:post_id>/comments`.

Summary

Our Post API is now a complete feature. If a developer wants, they can create a desktop or mobile application using this API, all without using HTML scraping, which is a very tedious and long process. Giving the developers who wish to use your website as a platform the ability to do so will increase your site's popularity, as they will essentially give you free advertising with their app or website.

In the next chapter, we will use the popular program Celery to run programs and tasks asynchronously with our application.

Creating Asynchronous Tasks with Celery

While creating web apps, it is vital to keep the time that a request takes to process below or around 50 ms. As the majority of response times are occupied by waiting for users' connection, and extra processing time may hang the server. Any extra processing on the server that can be avoided should be avoided. However, it is quite common for several operations in a web app to take longer than a couple of seconds, especially when complex database operations or image processing are involved. To save our user experience, a task queue named Celery will be used to move these operations out of the Flask process.

What is Celery?

Celery is an asynchronous task queue written in Python. Celery runs tasks, which are user-defined functions, *concurrently*—multiple tasks at once—through the Python multiprocessing library. Celery receives messages that tell it to start a task from a **broker**, which is usually called a message queue as shown in the following diagram:

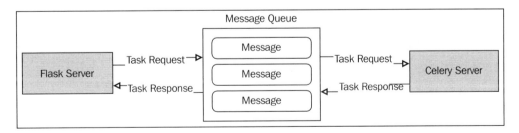

A **message queue** is a system specifically designed to send data between producer processes and consumer processes. **Producer processes** are any programs that create messages to be sent in the queue, and **consumer processes** are any programs that take the messages out of the queue. Messages sent from a producer are stored in a **First In First Out (FIFO)** queue, where the oldest items are retrieved first. Messages are stored until a consumer receives the message, after which it is deleted. Message queues provide real-time messaging without relying on polling, the process of continuously checking the status of a process. When messages are sent from producers, consumers are *listening* on their connection to the message queue for new messages; the consumer is not constantly contacting the queue. This difference is like the difference between **AJAX** and **WebSockets**; AJAX requires constant contact with the server while WebSockets are just a continuous stream.

It is possible to replace the message queue with a traditional database. Celery even comes with built-in support for SQLAlchemy to allow this. However, using a database as a broker for Celery is highly discouraged. Using a database in place of a message queue requires the consumer to constantly poll the database for updates. Also, because Celery uses multiprocessing for concurrency, the number of connections making lots of reads goes up quickly. Under medium loads, using a database requires the producer to make lots of writes to the database at the same time as the consumer is reading. Databases cannot have too many connections making reads, writes, and updates at the same time on the same data. When this happens, tables are often locked and all other connections are left waiting for each write to finish before anything can read the data, and vice versa. Even worse, it can lead to race conditions, which are situations where concurrent events change and read the same resource, and each concurrent operation started using a stale version of the data. Specific to Celery, this can lead to the same operation being run multiple times for the same message.

It is also possible to use a message queue as a broker and a database to store the results of the tasks. In the preceding diagram, the message queue was used for sending task requests and task results.

However, using a database to store the end result of the task allows the final product to be stored indefinitely, whereas the message queue will throw out the data as soon as the producer receives the data as shown in the following diagram:

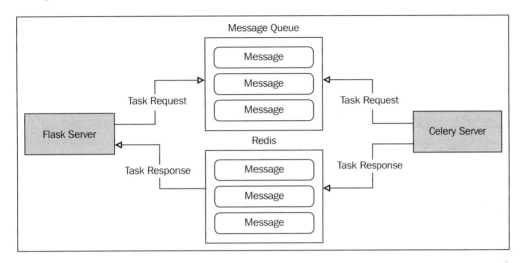

This database is often a key-value NoSQL store to help handle the load. This is useful if you plan on doing analytics on previously run tasks; otherwise, it's safer to just stick with the message queue.

There is even an option to drop the results of tasks entirely and not have the results of tasks returned. This has the downside that the producer has no way of knowing if a task was successful or not, but often this is enough in smaller projects.

For our stack, we will use **RabbitMQ** as the message broker. RabbitMQ runs on all major OSes and is very simple to set up and run. Celery also supports RabbitMQ without any extra libraries and is the recommended message queue in the Celery documentation.

> At the time of writing, there is no way to use RabbitMQ with Celery in Python 3. You can use Redis instead of RabbitMQ. The only difference will be the connection strings. For more information, see
> `http://docs.celeryproject.org/en/latest/getting-started/brokers/redis.html`.

Setting up Celery and RabbitMQ

To install Celery with `pip`, run the following:

```
$ pip install Celery
```

We will also need a Flask extension to help handle initializing Celery:

```
$ pip install Flask-Celery-Helper
```

The Flask documentation states that Flask extensions for Celery are unnecessary. However, getting the Celery server to work with Flask's application context when your app is organized with an application factory is significant. So, we will use **Flask-Celery-Helper** to do the heavy lifting.

Next, RabbitMQ needs to be installed. RabbitMQ is not written in Python; therefore, installation instructions will be different for every OS. Thankfully, RabbitMQ maintains a detailed list of instructions for each OS at `https://www.rabbitmq.com/download.html`.

After RabbitMQ is installed, go to a terminal window and run the following:

```
$ rabbitmq-server
```

This will start a RabbitMQ server with a user of guest and a password of guest. By default, RabbitMQ only accepts connections on localhost, so this setup is okay for the development.

Creating tasks in Celery

As stated before, Celery tasks are just user-defined functions that perform some operations. But before any tasks can be written, our Celery object needs to be created. This is the object that the Celery server will import to handle running and scheduling all of the tasks.

At a bare minimum, Celery needs one configuration variable to run: the connection to the message broker. The connection is defined like the SQLAlchemy connection, as a URL. The backend, what stores our tasks' results, is also defined as a URL as shown in the following code:

```python
class DevConfig(Config):
    DEBUG = True
    SQLALCHEMY_DATABASE_URI = 'sqlite:///../database.db'
    CELERY_BROKER_URL = "amqp://guest:guest@localhost:5672//"
```

```
CELERY_BACKEND = "amqp://guest:guest@localhost:5672//"
```

In the extensions.py file, the Celery class from Flask-Celery-Helper will be initialized:

```
from flask.ext.celery import Celery
celery = Celery()
```

So, in order for our Celery process to work with the database and any other Flask extensions, it needs to work within our application context. In order to do so, Celery will need to create a new instance of our application for each process. Unlike most Celery apps, we need a Celery factory to create an application instance and register our Celery instance on it. In a new file in the top-level directory, the same location where manage.py resides, named celery_runner.py, add the following:

```python
import os
from webapp import create_app
from celery import Celery
from webapp.tasks import log

def make_celery(app):
    celery = Celery(
        app.import_name,
        broker=app.config['CELERY_BROKER_URL'],
        backend=app.config['CELERY_BACKEND_URL']
    )
    celery.conf.update(app.config)
    TaskBase = celery.Task

    class ContextTask(TaskBase):
        abstract = True

        def __call__(self, *args, **kwargs):
            with app.app_context():
                return TaskBase.__call__(self, *args, **kwargs)

    celery.Task = ContextTask

    return celery

env = os.environ.get('WEBAPP_ENV', 'dev')
flask_app = create_app(
    'webapp.config.%sConfig' % env.capitalize()
)
celery = make_celery(flask_app)
```

What the `make_celery` function does is wraps every call to each Celery task in a Python `with` block. This makes sure that every call to any Flask extension will work as it is working with our app. Also, make sure not to name the Flask app instance `app`, as Celery tries to import any object named `app` or `celery` as the Celery application instance. So, naming your Flask object `app` will cause Celery to try to use it as a Celery object.

Now, we can write our first task. It will be a simple task to start with, one that just returns any string passed to it. In a new file in the application directory named `tasks.py`, add the following:

```
from webapp.extensions import celeryfrom webapp.extensions import
celery
@celery.task()
def log(msg):
    return msg
```

Now, the final piece of the puzzle is to run the Celery process, which is called a **worker**, in a new terminal window. Again, this is the process that will be listening to our message broker for commands to start new tasks:

```
$ celery worker -A celery_runner --loglevel=info
```

The `loglevel` flag is there, so you can see the confirmation that a task was received and its output was available in the terminal window.

Now, we can send commands to our Celery worker. Open the `manage.py` shell and import the `log` task:

```
>>> from webapp.tasks import log
>>> log("Message")
Message
>>> result = log.delay("Message")
```

The function can be called as if it were any other function; doing so will execute the function in the current process. However, calling the `delay` method on the task will send a message to the worker process to execute the function with the given arguments.

In the terminal window that is running the Celery worker, you should see something like the following:

```
Task tasks.log succeeded in 0.0005873600021s: 'Message'
```

With any asynchronous task, the `ready` method can be used to tell if the task has successfully completed. If true, the `get` method can be used to retrieve the result of the tasks.

```
>>> result.ready()
True
>>> result.get()
"Message"
```

The `get` method causes the current process to wait until the `ready` function returns `True` to retrieve the result. So, calling `get` immediately after calling the task essentially makes the task synchronous. Because of this, it's rather rare for tasks to actually return a value to the producer. The vast majority of tasks perform some operation and then exit.

When a task is run on the Celery worker, the state of the task can be accessed via the `state` attribute. This allows for a more fine-grained understanding of what the task is currently doing in the worker process. The available states are as follows:

- `FAILURE`: The task failed and all of the retries failed as well
- `PENDING`: The task has not yet been received by the worker
- `RECEIVED`: The task has been received by the worker and is not yet processing
- `RETRY`: The task failed and is waiting to be retried
- `REVOKED`: The task was stopped
- `STARTED`: The worker has started processing the task
- `SUCCESS`: The task completed successfully

In Celery, if a task fails, then the task can recall itself with the `retry` method as follows:

```
@celery.task(bind=True)
def task(self, param):
    try:
        some_code
    except Exception, e:
        self.retry(exc=e)
```

The `bind` parameter in the decorator function tells Celery to pass a reference to the task object as the first parameter in the function. Using the `self` parameter, the `retry` method can be called, which will rerun the task with the same parameters. There are several other parameters that can be passed to the function decorator to change the behavior of the task:

- `max_retries`: This is the maximum number of times the task can be retried before it is declared as failed.

- `default_retry_delay`: This is the time in seconds to wait before running the task again. It's a good idea to keep this at somewhere around a minute or so if you expect that the conditions that led to the task failing are transitory — for example, network errors.

- `rate_limit`: This specifies the total number of unique calls to this task that are allowed to run in a given interval. If the value is an integer, it is the total number of this task that is allowed to run per second. The value can also be a string in the form of *x/m* for *x* number of tasks per minute or *x/h* for *x* number of tasks per hour. For example, passing in *5/m* will only allow this task to be called five times a minute.

- `time_limit`: If specified, the task will be killed if it runs longer than this number of seconds.

- `ignore_result`: If the task's return value isn't used, then don't send it back.

It's a good idea to specify all of these for each task to avoid any chance that a task will not be run.

Running Celery tasks

The `delay` method is a shorthand version of the `apply_async` method, which is called in this format:

```
task.apply_async(
    args=[1, 2],
    kwargs={'kwarg1': '1', 'kwarg2': '2'}
)
```

However, the `args` keyword can be implicit:

```
apply_async([1, 2], kwargs={'kwarg1': '1', 'kwarg2': '2'})
```

Calling `apply_async` allows you to define some extra functionality in the task call that you cannot specify in the `delay` method. First, the `countdown` option specifies the amount of time in seconds the worker should wait to run the task after receiving it:

```
>>> from webapp.tasks import log
>>> log.apply_async(["Message"], countdown=600)
```

`countdown` is not a guarantee that the task will be run after `600` seconds. `countdown` only says that the task is up for processing after *x* number of seconds. If all of the worker processes are busy with the other tasks, then it will not be run immediately.

Another keyword argument that `apply_async` gives is the `eta` argument. `eta` is passed through a Python `datetime` object that specifies exactly when the task should be run. Again, `eta` is not reliable.

```
>>> import datetime
>>> from webapp.tasks import log
# Run the task one hour from now
>>> eta = datetime.datetime.now() + datetime.timedelta(hours=1)
>>> log.apply_async(["Message"], eta=eta)
```

Celery workflows

Celery provides many ways to group multiple, dependent tasks together or to execute many tasks in parallel. These methods take a large amount of influence from language features found in functional programming languages. However, to understand how this works, we first need to understand signatures. Consider the following task:

```
@celery.task()
def multiply(x, y):
    return x * y
```

Let's see a **signature** in action to understand it. Open up the `manage.py` shell:

```
>>> from celery import signature
>>> from webapp.tasks import multiply
# Takes the same keyword args as apply_async
>>> signature('webapp.tasks.multiply', args=(4, 4) , countdown=10)
webapp.tasks.multiply(4, 4)
# same as above
```

```
>>> from webapp.tasks import multiply
>>> multiply.subtask((4, 4), countdown=10)
webapp.tasks.multiply(4, 4)
# shorthand for above, like delay in that it doesn't take
# apply_async's keyword args
>>> multiply.s(4, 4)
webapp.tasks.multiply(4, 4)
>>> multiply.s(4, 4)()
16
>>> multiply.s(4, 4).delay()
```

Calling a signature, or sometimes called a **subtask**, of a task creates a function that can be passed to the other functions to be executed. Executing the signature, like the third-to-last line in the example, executes the function in the current process and not in the worker.

Partials

The first application of task signatures is functional programming style partials. **Partials** are functions that originally take many arguments; however an operation is applied to the original function to return a new function, so the first *n* arguments are always the same. An example would be a `multiply` function that is not a task:

```
>>> new_multiply = multiply(2)
>>> new_multiply(5)
10
# The first function is unaffected
>>> multiply(2, 2)
4
```

This is a fictional API, but this is very close to the Celery version:

```
>>> partial = multiply.s(4)
>>> partial.delay(4)
```

The output in the worker window should show **16**. Basically, we created a new function that was saved to partial and that will always multiply its input by four.

Callbacks

Once a task is completed, it is very common to have another task run based on the output of the previous tasks. To achieve this, the apply_async function has a link method:

```
>>> multiply.apply_async((4, 4), link=log.s())
```

The worker output should show that both the multiply task and the log task returned **16**.

If you have a function that does not take input, or your callback does not need the result of the original method, the task signature must be marked as immutable with the si method:

```
>>> multiply.apply_async((4, 4), link=log.si("Message"))
```

Callbacks can be used to solve real-world problems. If we wanted to send a welcome e-mail every time a task created a new user, then we could produce that effect with the following call:

```
>>> create_user.apply_async(("John Doe", password), link=welcome.s())
```

Partials and callbacks can be combined to produce some powerful effects:

```
>>> multiply.apply_async((4, 4), link=multiply.s(4))
```

It's important to note that if this call was saved and the get method was called on it, the result would be **16** rather than **64**. This is because the get method does not return the results for callback methods. This will be solved with later methods.

Group

The group function takes a list of signatures and creates a callable function to execute all of the signatures in parallel and then return a list of all of the results:

```
>>> from celery import group
>>> sig = group(multiply.s(i, i+5) for i in range(10))
>>> result = sig.delay()
>>> result.get()
[0, 6, 14, 24, 36, 50, 66, 84, 104, 126]
```

Chain

The `chain` function takes task signatures and passes the value of each result to the next value in the chain, returning one result as follows:

```
>>> from celery import chain
>>> sig = chain(multiply.s(10, 10), multiply.s(4), multiply.s(20))
# same as above
>>> sig = (multiply.s(10, 10) | multiply.s(4) | multiply.s(20))
>>> result = sig.delay()
>>> result.get()
8000
```

Chains and partials can be taken a bit further. Chains can be used to create new functions when using partials, and chains can be nested as follows:

```
# combining partials in chains
>>> func = (multiply.s(10) | multiply.s(2))
>>> result = func.delay(16)
>>> result.get()
200
# chains can be nested
>>> func = (
    multiply.s(10) | multiply.s(2) | (multiply.s(4) | multiply.s(5))
)
>>> result = func.delay(16)
>>> result.get()
800
```

Chord

The `chord` function creates a signature that will execute a `group` of signatures and pass the final result to a callback:

```
>>> from celery import chord
>>> sig = chord(
    group(multiply.s(i, i+5) for i in range(10)),
    log.s()
)
```

```
>>> result = sig.delay()
>>> result.get()
[0, 6, 14, 24, 36, 50, 66, 84, 104, 126]
```

Just like the link argument, the callback is not returned with the `get` method.

Using the `chain` syntax with a group and a callback automatically creates a chord signature:

```
# same as above
>>> sig = (group(multiply.s(i, i+5) for i in range(10)) | log.s())
>>> result = sig.delay()
>>> result.get()
[0, 6, 14, 24, 36, 50, 66, 84, 104, 126]
```

Running tasks periodically

Celery also has the ability to call tasks periodically. For those familiar with ***nix** OSes, this system is a lot like the command-line utility `cron`, but it has the added benefit of being defined in our source code rather than on some system file. As such, it will be much easier to update when our code is ready for publishing to production in *Chapter 13, Deploying Flask Apps,*. In addition, all of the tasks are run within the application context, whereas a Python script called by `cron` would not be.

To add periodic tasks, add the following to the `DevConfig` configuration object:

```
import datetime

...

CELERYBEAT_SCHEDULE = {
    'log-every-30-seconds': {
        'task': 'webapp.tasks.log',
        'schedule': datetime.timedelta(seconds=30),
        'args': ("Message",)
    },
}
```

This `configuration` variable defines that the `log` task should be run every 30 seconds with the `args` tuple passed as the parameters. Any `timedelta` object can be used to define the interval to run the task on.

To run periodic tasks, another specialized worker named a `beat` worker is needed. In another terminal window, run the following:

```
$ celery -A celery_runner beat
```

If you now watch the terminal output in the main `Celery` worker, you should now see a log event every 30 seconds.

What if your task needs to run at much more specific intervals, for example, every Tuesday in June at 3 am and 5 pm? For very specific intervals, there is the Celery `crontab` object.

To illustrate how the `crontab` object represents intervals, here are some examples:

```
>>> from celery.schedules import crontab
# Every midnight
>>> crontab(minute=0, hour=0)
# Once a 5AM, then 10AM, then 3PM, then 8PM
>>> crontab(minute=0, hour=[5, 10, 15, 20])
# Every half hour
>>> crontab(minute='*/30')
# Every Monday at even numbered hours and 1AM
>>> crontab(day_of_week=1, hour ='*/2, 1')
```

The object has the following arguments:

- `minute`
- `hour`
- day_of_week
- `day_of_month`
- `month_of_year`

Each of these arguments can take various inputs. With plain integers, they operate much like the `timedelta` object, but they can also take strings and lists. When passed a list, the task will execute on every moment that is in the list. When passed a string in the form of */x, the task will execute every moment that the modulo operation returns zero. Also, the two forms can be combined to form a comma-separated string of integers and divisions.

Monitoring Celery

When our code is pushed to the server, our `Celery` worker will not be run in the terminal window, it will be run as a background task. Because of this, Celery provides many command-line arguments to monitor the status of your `Celery` worker and tasks. These commands take the following form:

```
$ celery -A celery_runner <command>
```

The main tasks to view the status of your workers are as follows:

- `status`: This prints the running workers and if they are up
- `result`: When passed a task id, this shows the return value and final status of the task
- `purge`: Using this, all messages in the broker will be deleted
- `inspect active`: This lists all active tasks
- `inspect scheduled`: This lists all tasks that have been scheduled with the `eta` argument
- `inspect registered`: This lists all of the tasks waiting to be processed
- `inspect stats`: This returns a dictionary full of statistics on the currently running workers and the broker

Web-based monitoring with Flower

Flower is a web-based, real-time management tool for Celery. In Flower, all active, queued, and completed tasks can be monitored. Flower also provides graphs and stats on how long each graph has been sitting in the queue versus how long its execution took and the arguments to each of those tasks.

To install Flower, use `pip` as follows:

```
$ pip install flower
```

To run it, just treat `flower` as a Celery command as follows:

```
$ celery flower -A celery_runner --loglevel=info
```

Now, open your browser to `http://localhost:5555`. It's best to familiarize yourself with the interface while tasks are running, so go to the command line and type the following:

```
>>> sig = chord(
    group(multiply.s(i, i+5) for i in xrange(10000)),
    log.s()
)

>>> sig.delay()
```

Your worker process will now start processing 10,000 tasks. Browse around the different pages while the tasks are running to see how Flower interacts with your worker while it is really churning.

Creating a reminder app

Let's get into some real-world examples in Celery. Suppose another page on our site now requires a reminder feature. Users can create reminders that will send an e-mail to a specified location at the time specified. We will need a model, a task, and a way to call our task automatically every time a model is created.

Let's start with the following basic SQLAlchemy model:

```
class Reminder(db.Model):
    id = db.Column(db.Integer(), primary_key=True)
    date = db.Column(db.DateTime())
    email = db.Column(db.String())
    text = db.Column(db.Text())

    def __repr__(self):
        return "<Reminder '{}'>".format(self.text[:20])
```

Now we need a task that will send an e-mail to the location in the model. In our `tasks.py` file, add the following task:

```
import smtplib
from email.mime.text import MIMEText

@celery.task(
    bind=True,
    ignore_result=True,
```

```
        default_retry_delay=300,
        max_retries=5
    )
def remind(self, pk):
    reminder = Reminder.query.get(pk)
    msg = MIMEText(reminder.text)

    msg['Subject'] = "Your reminder"
    msg['From'] = your_email
    msg['To'] = reminder.email

    try:
        smtp_server = smtplib.SMTP('localhost')
        smtp_server.starttls()
        smtp_server.login(user, password)
        smtp_server.sendmail(
            your_email,
            [reminder.email],
            msg.as_string()
        )
        smtp_server.close()

        return
    except Exception, e:
        self.retry(exc=e)
```

Note that our task takes a primary key rather than a model. This is a hedge against a race condition, as a passed model could be stale by the time the worker finally gets around to processing it. You will also have to replace the placeholder e-mails and login with your own login info.

How do we have our task called when the user creates a reminder model? We will use a SQLAlchemy feature named `events`. SQLAlchemy allows us to register callbacks on our models that will be called when specific changes are made to our models. Our task will use the `after_insert` event, which is called after new data is entered into the database, whether the model is brand new or being updated.

We need a callback in `tasks.py`:

```
def on_reminder_save(mapper, connect, self):
    remind.apply_async(args=(self.id,), eta=self.date)
```

Now, in `__init__.py`, we will register our callback on our model:

```
from sqlalchemy import event
from .tasks import on_reminder_save

def create_app(object_name):
    app = Flask(__name__)
    app.config.from_object(object_name)

    db.init_app(app)
    event.listen(Reminder, 'after_insert', on_reminder_save)
    ...
```

Now, every time a model is saved, a task is registered that will send an e-mail to our user.

Creating a weekly digest

Say our blog has a lot of people who don't use RSS and prefer mailing lists, which is a large number of users. We need some way to create a list of new posts at the end of every week to increase our site's traffic. To solve this problem, we will create a digest task that will be called by a beat worker at 10 am every Saturday.

First, in `tasks.py`, let's create our task as follows:

```
@celery.task(
    bind=True,
    ignore_result=True,
    default_retry_delay=300,
    max_retries=5
)
def digest(self):
    # find the start and end of this week
    year, week = datetime.datetime.now().isocalendar()[0:2]
    date = datetime.date(year, 1, 1)
    if (date.weekday() > 3):
        date = date + datetime.timedelta(days=7 - date.weekday())
    else:
        date = date - datetime.timedelta(days=date.weekday())
    delta = datetime.timedelta(days=(week - 1) * 7)
```

```
    start, end = date + delta, date + delta +
        datetime.timedelta(days=6)

    posts = Post.query.filter(
        Post.publish_date >= start,
        Post.publish_date <= end
    ).all()

    if (len(posts) == 0):
        return

    msg = MIMEText(
        render_template("digest.html", posts=posts),
        'html'
    )

    msg['Subject'] = "Weekly Digest"
    msg['From'] = your_email

    try:
        smtp_server = smtplib.SMTP('localhost')
        smtp_server.starttls()
        smtp_server.login(user, password)
        smtp_server.sendmail(
            your_email,
            [recipients],
            msg.as_string()
        )
        smtp_server.close()

        return
    except Exception, e:
        self.retry(exc=e)
```

We will also need to add a periodic schedule to our configuration object in `config.py` to manage our task:

```
CELERYBEAT_SCHEDULE = {
    'weekly-digest': {
        'task': 'tasks.digest',
        'schedule': crontab(day_of_week=6, hour='10')
    },
}
```

Finally, we need our e-mail template. Unfortunately, HTML in e-mail clients is terribly outdated. Every single e-mail client has different rendering bugs and quirks, and the only way to find them is to open your e-mail in all the clients. Many e-mail clients don't even support CSS, and those that do support a very small amount of selectors and attributes. In order to compensate, we have to use the web development methods of 10 years ago, that is, designing with tables with inline styles. Here is our `digest.html`:

```
"http://www.w3.org/TR/xhtml1/DTD/xhtml1-transitional.dtd">
<html xmlns="http://www.w3.org/1999/xhtml">
    <head>
        <meta http-equiv="Content-Type"
            content="text/html; charset=UTF-8" />
        <meta name="viewport"
            content="width=device-width, initial-scale=1.0"/>
        <title>Weekly Digest</title>
    </head>
    <body>
        <table align="center"
            border="0"
            cellpadding="0"
            cellspacing="0"
            width="500px">
        <tr>
            <td style="font-size: 32px;
                    font-family: Helvetica, sans-serif;
                    color: #444;
                    text-align: center;
                    line-height: 1.65">
                Weekly Digest
            </td>
        </tr>
        {% for post in posts %}
            <tr>
                <td style="font-size: 24px;
                        font-family: sans-serif;
                        color: #444;
                        text-align: center;
                        line-height: 1.65">
                    {{ post.title }}
                </td>
```

```
            </tr>
            <tr>
                <td style="font-size: 14px;
                            font-family: serif;
                            color: #444;
                            line-height:1.65">
                    {{ post.text | truncate(500) | safe }}
                </td>
            </tr>
            <tr>
                <td style="font-size: 12px;
                            font-family: serif;
                            color: blue;
                            margin-bottom: 20px">
                    <a href="{{ url_for('.post',
                        post_id=post.id) }}">Read More</a>
                </td>
            </tr>
        {% endfor %}
        </table>
    </body>
</html>
```

Now, at the end of every week, our digest task will be called and it will send an e-mail to all the users present in our mailing list.

Summary

Celery is a very powerful task queue that allows programmers to defer the processing of slower tasks to another process. Now that you understand how to move complex tasks out of the Flask process, we will take a look at a collection of Flask extensions that simplify some common tasks seen in Flask apps.

10
Useful Flask Extensions

As we have seen throughout this book, Flask is designed to be as small as possible while still giving you the flexibility and tools needed to create web applications. However, there are a lot of features that are common to many web applications, which means that many applications will require writing code that does the same task for each web application. To solve this problem, people have created extensions to Flask to avoid reinventing the wheel, and we have seen many Flask extensions already throughout the book. This chapter will focus on some of the more useful Flask extensions that don't have enough content to separate them out into their own chapter, but will save you a lot of time and frustration.

Flask Script

In *Chapter 1*, *Getting Started*, we created a basic manage script with the Flask extension Flask Script to allow easy running of the server and debugging with the shell. In this chapter, we will cover the features that were not covered in that basic introduction.

In Flask Script, you can create custom commands to be run within the application context. All that is needed is to create a command to decorate a normal Python function with a decorator function provided by Flask Script. For example, if we wanted a task that would return the string "Hello, World!" we would add the following to `manage.py`:

```python
@manager.command
def test():
    print "Hello, World!"
```

From the command line, the `test` command can now be run using the following:

```
$ python manage.py test
Hello, World!
```

Delete the test command, and let's create a simple command to help set up new developers on our application by creating their SQLite database and filling it with test data. This command is partially lifted from the script created in *Chapter 4, Creating Controllers with Blueprints*:

```python
@manager.command
def setup_db():
    db.create_all()

    admin_role = Role()
    admin_role.name = "admin"
    admin_role.description = "admin"
    db.session.add(admin_role)

    default_role = Role()
    default_role.name = "default"
    default_role.description = "default"
    db.session.add(default_role)

    admin = User()
    admin.username = "admin"
    admin.set_password("password")
    admin.roles.append(admin_role)
    admin.roles.append(default_role)
    db.session.add(admin)

    tag_one = Tag('Python')
    tag_two = Tag('Flask')
    tag_three = Tag('SQLAlechemy')
    tag_four = Tag('Jinja')
    tag_list = [tag_one, tag_two, tag_three, tag_four]

    s = "Body text"

    for i in xrange(100):
        new_post = Post("Post {}".format(i))
        new_post.user = admin
```

```
new_post.publish_date = datetime.datetime.now()
new_post.text = s
new_post.tags = random.sample(
    tag_list,
    random.randint(1, 3)
)
db.session.add(new_post)

db.session.commit()
```

Now if a new developer is assigned the project, they could download the `git repo` from our server, install the `pip` libraries, run the `setup_db` command, and would be able to run the project with everything they need.

Flask Script also provides two utility functions that can be easily added to our project.

```
from flask.ext.script.commands import ShowUrls, Clean
...
manager = Manager(app)
manager.add_command("server", Server())
manager.add_command("show-urls", ShowUrls())
manager.add_command("clean", Clean())
```

The `show-urls` command lists all of the routes registered on the `app` object and the URL tied to that route. This is very useful while debugging Flask extensions, as it becomes trivial to see whether the registration of its blueprints is working or not. The Clean command just removes the `.pyc` and `.pyo` compiled Python files from our working directory.

Flask Debug Toolbar

Flask Debug Toolbar is a Flask extension that aids development by adding debugging tools into the web view of your application. It gives you information such as the bottlenecks in your view rendering code, and how many SQLAlchemy queries it took to render the view.

As always, we will use `pip` to install Flask Debug Toolbar:

```
$ pip install flask-debugtoolbar
```

Next, we need to add Flask Debug Toolbar to the `extensions.py` file. As we will be modifying this file a lot in this chapter, here is the start of the file so far along with the code to initialize Flask Debug Toolbar:

```
from flask import flash, redirect, url_for, session
from flask.ext.bcrypt import Bcrypt
from flask.ext.openid import OpenID
from flask_oauth import OAuth
from flask.ext.login import LoginManager
from flask.ext.principal import Principal, Permission, RoleNeed
from flask.ext.restful import Api
from flask.ext.celery import Celery
from flask.ext.debugtoolbar import DebugToolbarExtension

bcrypt = Bcrypt()
oid = OpenID()
oauth = OAuth()
principals = Principal()
celery = Celery()
debug_toolbar = DebugToolbarExtension()
```

Now, the initialization function needs to be called in our `create_app` function in `__init__.py`:

```
from .extensions import (
    bcrypt,
    oid,
    login_manager,
    principals,
    rest_api,
    celery,
    debug_toolbar,
)


def create_app(object_name):

    debug_toolbar.init_app(app)
```

This is all that is needed to get Flask Debug Toolbar up and running. If the DEBUG variable in your app's config is set to *true*, the toolbar will appear. If DEBUG is not set to *true*, the toolbar will not be injected into the page.

On the right-hand side of the screen, you will see the toolbar. Each section is a link that will display a table of values on the page. To get a list of all the functions that were called in order to render the view, click the checkmark next to **Profiler** to enable it, reload the page, and click on **Profiler**. This view easily allows you to quickly diagnose which parts of your apps are the slowest or are called the most.

By default, Flask Debug Toolbar intercepts HTTP 302 redirect requests. To disable this, add the following to your configuration:

```
class DevConfig(Config):
    DEBUG = True
    DEBUG_TB_INTERCEPT_REDIRECTS = False
```

Also, if you are using Flask-MongoEngine, you can view all of the queries that were made to render the page by overriding which panels are rendered and adding MongoEngine's custom panel.

```
class DevConfig(Config):
    DEBUG = True
    DEBUG_TB_PANELS = [
        'flask_debugtoolbar.panels.versions.VersionDebugPanel',
        'flask_debugtoolbar.panels.timer.TimerDebugPanel',
        'flask_debugtoolbar.panels.headers.HeaderDebugPanel',
        'flask_debugtoolbar.panels.
        request_vars.RequestVarsDebugPanel',
        'flask_debugtoolbar.panels.config_vars.
        ConfigVarsDebugPanel ',
        'flask_debugtoolbar.panels.template.
        TemplateDebugPanel',
        'flask_debugtoolbar.panels.
        logger.LoggingPanel',
        'flask_debugtoolbar.panels.
        route_list.RouteListDebugPanel'
        'flask_debugtoolbar.panels.profiler.
        ProfilerDebugPanel',
        'flask.ext.mongoengine.panels.
        MongoDebugPanel'
    ]
    DEBUG_TB_INTERCEPT_REDIRECTS = False
```

This will add a panel to the toolbar that is very similar to the default SQLAlchemy one.

Flask Cache

In *Chapter 7, Using NoSQL with Flask*, we learned that page load time is one of the most important factors to determine the success of your web app. Despite the fact that our pages do not change very often and due to the fact that new posts will not be made very often, we still render the template and query the database every single time the page is asked for by our user's browsers.

Flask Cache solves this problem by allowing us to store the results of our view functions and return the stored results rather than render the template again. First, we need to install Flask Cache from `pip`:

```
$ pip install Flask-Cache
```

Next, initialize it in `extensions.py`:

```
from flask.ext.cache import Cache

cache = Cache()
```

Then, register the `Cache` object on the application, in the `create_app` function in `__init__.py`:

```
from .extensions import (
    bcrypt,
    oid,
    login_manager,
    principals,
    rest_api,
    celery,
    debug_toolbar,
    cache
)

def create_app(object_name):
    ...
    cache.init_app(app)
```

Before we can start caching our views, there is a need to tell Flash Cache how we want to store the results of our new functions.

```
class DevConfig(Config):
    ...
    CACHE_TYPE = 'simple'
```

The `simple` option tells Flask Cache to store the results in memory in a Python dictionary, which for the vast majority of Flask apps is adequate. We'll cover more types of Cache backends later in this section.

Caching views and functions

In order to cache the results of a view function, simply add a decorator to any function:

```
@blog_blueprint.route('/')
@blog_blueprint.route('/<int:page>')
@cache.cached(timeout=60)
def home(page=1):
```

```
posts = Post.query.order_by(
    Post.publish_date.desc()
).paginate(page, 10)
recent, top_tags = sidebar_data()

return render_template(
    'home.html',
    posts=posts,
    recent=recent,
    top_tags=top_tags
)
```

The `timeout` parameter specifies how many seconds the cached result should last before the function should be run again and stored again. To confirm that the view is actually being cached, check the SQLAlchemy section on the Debug Toolbar. Also, we can see that the impact caching has on page load times by activating the profiler and comparing the times before and after. On the author's top of the line laptop, the main blog page takes 34 ms to render, mainly due to the eight different queries that are made to the database. But after the cache is activated, this decreases to .08 ms. That's a 462.5 percent increase in speed!

View functions are not the only thing that can be cached. To cache any Python function, simply add a similar decorator to the function definition as follows:

```
@cache.cached(timeout=7200, key_prefix='sidebar_data')
def sidebar_data():
    recent = Post.query.order_by(
        Post.publish_date.desc()
    ).limit(5).all()

    top_tags = db.session.query(
        Tag, func.count(tags.c.post_id).label('total')
    ).join(
        tags
    ).group_by(
        Tag
    ).order_by('total DESC').limit(5).all()

    return recent, top_tags
```

The keyword argument `key_prefix` is necessary for non view functions in order for Flask Cache to properly store the results of the function. This needs to be unique for every function cached, or the results of the functions will override each other. Also, note that the timeout for this function is set to 2 hours rather than the 60 seconds in the previous examples. This is because the results for this function are less likely to change than the view functions, and if the data is stale, it is not as big an issue.

Caching functions with parameters

However, the normal cache decorator does not take function parameters into account. If we cached a function that took parameters with the normal cache decorator, it would return the same result for every parameter set. In order to fix this, we use the `memoize` function:

```
class User(db.Model):

    ...


    @staticmethod
    @cache.memoize(60)
    def verify_auth_token(token):
        s = Serializer(current_app.config['SECRET_KEY'])

        try:
            data = s.loads(token)
        except SignatureExpired:
            return None
        except BadSignature:
            return None

        user = User.query.get(data['id'])
        return user
```

`Memoize` stores the parameters passed to the function as well as the result. In the preceding example, `memoize` is being used to store the result of the `verify_auth_token` method, which is called many times and queries the database every single time. This method can safely be memoized because it returns the same result every time if the same token is passed to it. The only exception to this rule is if the user object gets deleted during the 60 seconds that the function is stored, but this is very unlikely.

Be careful not to `memoize` or cache functions that rely on either globally scoped variables or on constantly changing data. This can lead to some very subtle bugs, and in the worst case, data race. The best candidates for memoization are what are referred to as pure functions. Pure functions are functions that will produce the same result when the same parameters are passed to them. It does not matter how many times the function is run. Pure functions also do not have any side effects, which means that they do not change globally scoped variables. This also means that pure functions cannot do any IO operations. While the `verify_auth_token` function is not pure because it does database IO, it is ok because as was stated before it is very unlikely that the underlying data will change.

While we are developing the application, we do not want the view functions to be cached because results will be changing all the time. To fix this, set the CACHE_TYPE variable to null and set the CACHE_TYPE variable to simple in the production configuration, so when the app is deployed everything works as expected:

```
class ProdConfig(Config):
    ...
    CACHE_TYPE = 'simple'


class DevConfig(Config):
    ...
    CACHE_TYPE = 'null'
```

Caching routes with query strings

Some routes, such as our home and post routes, take the parameters through the URL and return content specific to those parameters. We run into a problem if routes like these are cached, as the first rendering of the route will be returned for all requests regardless of the URL parameters. The solution is rather simple. The key_prefix keyword argument in the cache method can be either a string or a function, which will be executed to dynamically generate a key. This means that a function can be created to generate a key that is tied to the URL parameters, so each request only returns a cached page if that specific combination of parameters has been called before. In the blog.py file, add the following:

```
def make_cache_key(*args, **kwargs):
    path = request.path
    args = str(hash(frozenset(request.args.items())))
    lang = get_locale()
    return (path + args + lang).encode('utf-8')



@blog_blueprint.route(
    '/post/<int:post_id>',
    methods=('GET', 'POST')
)
@cache.cached(timeout=600, key_prefix=make_cache_key)
def post(post_id):
    ...
```

Now, each individual post page will be cached for 10 minutes.

Using Redis as a cache backend

If the amount of view functions or the number of unique parameters passed to your cached functions becomes too large for memory, you can use a different backend for the cache. As was mentioned in *Chapter 7, Using NoSQL with Flask*, Redis can be used as a backend for the cache. To implement that functionality, all that needs to be done is to add the following configuration variables to the `ProdConfig` class as follows:

```
class ProdConfig(Config):
    ...
    CACHE_TYPE = 'redis'
    CACHE_REDIS_HOST = 'localhost'
    CACHE_REDIS_PORT = '6379'
    CACHE_REDIS_PASSWORD = 'password'
    CACHE_REDIS_DB = '0'
```

If you replace the values of the variables with your own data, Flask Cache will automatically create a connection to your `redis` database and use it to store the results of the functions. All that is needed is to install the Python `redis` library:

```
$ pip install redis
```

Using memcached as a cache backend

Just like the `redis` backend, the `memcached` backend provides an alternative way of storing results if the memory option is too limiting. In contrast to `redis`, `memcached` is designed to `cache` objects for later use and reduce load on the database. Both `redis` and `memcached` can serve the same purpose, and choosing one over the other comes down to personal preference. To use `memcached`, we need to install its Python library:

```
$ pip install memcache
```

Connecting to your `memcached` server is handled in the configuration object, just like the `redis` setup:

```
class ProdConfig(Config):
    ...
    CACHE_TYPE = 'memcached'
    CACHE_KEY_PREFIX = 'flask_cache'
    CACHE_MEMCACHED_SERVERS = ['localhost:11211']
```

Flask Assets

Another bottleneck in web applications are the amount of HTTP requests required to download the CSS and JavaScript libraries for the page. The extra files can only be downloaded after HTML for the page has been loaded and parsed. To combat this, many modern browsers download many of these libraries at once, but there is a limit to how many simultaneous requests the browser makes.

Several things can be done on the server to reduce the amount of time spent downloading these files. The main technique that developers use is to concatenate all of the JavaScript libraries into one file and all of the CSS libraries into another while removing all of the whitespace and carriage returns from the resulting files. This reduces the overhead of multiple HTTP requests, and removing the unnecessary whitespace and carriage returns can reduce a file's size by up to 30 percent. Another technique is to tell the browser to cache the files locally with specialized HTTP headers, so the file is only loaded again once it changes. These can be tedious to do manually because they need to be done after every deployment to the server.

Thankfully, Flask Assets implements all the above techniques. Flask Assets works by giving it a list of files and a way to concatenate them, and then adding a special control block into your templates in place of the normal link and script tags. Flask Assets will then add in a link or a script tag that links to the newly generated file. To get started, Flask Assets needs to be installed. We also need to install `cssmin` and `jsmin`, which are Python libraries that handle the modification of the files:

```
$ pip install Flask-Assets cssmin jsmin
```

Now, the collections of files to be concatenated, named bundles, need to be created. In `extensions.py`, add the following:

```python
from flask_assets import Environment, Bundle

assets_env = Environment()

main_css = Bundle(
    'css/bootstrap.css',
    filters='cssmin',
    output='css/common.css'
)

main_js = Bundle(
    'js/jquery.js',
    'js/bootstrap.js',
    filters='jsmin',
    output='js/common.js'
)
```

Each `Bundle` object takes an infinite number of files as positional arguments to define the files to be bundled, a keyword argument `filters` to define the filters to send the files through, and an `output` that defines the filename in the `static` folder to save the result to.

> The `filters` keyword can be a single value or a list. To get the full list of available filters, including automatic Less and CSS compliers, see the docs at `http://webassets.readthedocs.org/en/latest/`.

While it's true that because our site is light on styles the CSS bundle has only one file in it. It's still a good idea to put the file in a bundle for two reasons.

While we are in development, we can use the un-minified versions of the libraries, which makes debugging easier. When the app is deployed to production, the libraries are automatically minified.

These libraries will be sent to the browser with the cache headers, when linking them in HTML normally would not.

Before Flask Assets can be tested, three more changes need to be made. First, in the `__init__.py` format, the extension and bundles need to be registered:

```
from .extensions import (
    bcrypt,
    oid,
    login_manager,
    principals,
    rest_api,
    celery,
    debug_toolbar,
    cache,
    assets_env,
    main_js,
    main_css
)


def create_app(object_name):
    ...
    assets_env.init_app(app)

    assets_env.register("main_js", main_js)
    assets_env.register("main_css", main_css)
```

Next, the `DevConfig` class needs an extra variable to tell Flask Assets to not compile the libraries while in development:

```
class DevConfig(Config):
    DEBUG = True
    DEBUG_TB_INTERCEPT_REDIRECTS = False

    ASSETS_DEBUG = True
```

Finally, the link and script tags in both of the `base.html` files need to be replaced with the control block from Flask Assets. We have the following:

```
<link rel="stylesheet"
href=https://maxcdn.bootstrapcdn.com/bootstrap/3.3.2/css/bootst
rap.min.css>
```

Replace this with the following:

```
{% assets "main_css" %}
<link rel="stylesheet" type="text/css" href="{{ ASSET_URL }}"
/>
{% endassets %}
```

We also have the following:

```
<script
src="https://ajax.googleapis.com/ajax/libs/jquery/1.11.2/jquery
.min.js"></script>
<script
src="https://maxcdn.bootstrapcdn.com/bootstrap/3.3.2/js/bootstr
ap.min.js"></script>
```

Replace this with the following:

```
{% assets "main_js" %}
<script src="{{ ASSET_URL }}"></script>
{% endassets %}
```

Now, if you reload the page, all of the CSS and JavaScript will now be handled by Flask Assets.

Flask Admin

In *Chapter 6, Securing Your App*, we created an interface to allow users to create and edit blog posts without having to use the command line. This was adequate to demonstrate the security measures presented in the chapter, but there is still no way for posts to be deleted or tags assigned to them using the interface. We also do not have a way to delete or edit comments that we would rather not have common users see. What our app needs is a fully featured administrator interface in the same vein as the WordPress interface. This is such a common requirement for apps that a Flask extension name Flask Admin was created to easily create administrator interfaces. To get started, install Flask Admin with `pip`:

```
$ pip install Flask-Admin
```

As usual, we need to create the `extension` object in `extensions.py`:

```
from flask.ext.admin import Admin

admin = Admin()
```

Then, the object needs to be registered on the `app` object in `__init__.py`:

```
from .extensions import (
    bcrypt,
    oid,
    login_manager,
    principals,
    rest_api,
    celery,
    debug_toolbar,
    cache,
    assets_env,
    main_js,
    main_css,
    admin
)

def create_app(object_name):
    ...
    admin.init_app(app)
```

If you navigate to `localhost:5000/admin`, you should now see the empty Flask Admin interface:

Flask Admin works by registering view classes on the `admin` object that define one or more routes. Flask Admin has three main types of views: the `ModelView`, `FileAdmin`, and `BaseView` views.

Creating basic admin pages

The `BaseView` class allows normal Flask pages to be added to your `admin` interface. This is normally the least used type of view in Flask Admin setups, but if you wish to include something like custom reporting with JavaScript charting libraries, you would do it with just a base view. In a new file in the controllers folder named `admin.py`, add the following:

```
from flask.ext.admin import BaseView, expose

class CustomView(BaseView):
    @expose('/')
    def index(self):
        return self.render('admin/custom.html')

    @expose('/second_page')
    def second_page(self):
        return self.render('admin/second_page.html')
```

In a subclass of `BaseView`, multiple views can be registered at once if they are defined together. Keep in mind, however, that each subclass of `BaseView` requires at least one exposed method on the path /. Also, methods other than the method within the path / will not be in the navigation of the administrator interface, and will have to be linked to the other pages in the class. The `expose` and `self.render` functions work exactly the same as their counterparts in the normal Flask API.

To have your templates inherit the default styles of Flask Admin, create a new folder in the templates directory named `admin` with a file named `custom.html` and add the following Jinja code:

```
{% extends 'admin/master.html' %}
{% block body %}
    This is the custom view!
    <a href="{{ url_for('.second_page') }}">Link</a>
{% endblock %}
```

To view this template, an instance of `CustomView` needs to be registered on the `admin` object. This will be done in the `create_app` function rather than in the `extensions.py` file because some of our admin pages will need the database object, which would lead to circular imports if the registrations were in `extensions.py`. In `__init__.py`, add the following code to register the class:

```
from webapp.controllers.admin import CustomView

...

def create_app(object_name):

    ...

    admin.add_view(CustomView(name='Custom'))
```

The `name` keyword argument specifies that the label used in the navigation bar on the top of the `admin` interface should read `Custom`. After you have registered `CustomView` to the `admin` object, your `admin` interface should now have a second link in the navigation bar as follows.

Creating database admin pages

The main power of Flask Admin comes from the fact that you can automatically create administrator pages for your data by giving Flask Admin your SQLAlchemy or MongoEngine models. Creating these pages is very easy; in `admin.py`, just add the following code:

```
from flask.ext.admin.contrib.sqla import ModelView
# or, if you use MongoEngine
from flask.ext.admin.contrib.mongoengine import ModelView

class CustomModelView(ModelView):
    pass
```

Then, in `__init__.py`, register the class with the model you wish to use and the database `session` object as follows:

```
from controllers.admin import CustomView, CustomModelView
from .models import db, Reminder, User, Role, Post, Comment, Tag

def create_app(object_name):

    admin.add_view(CustomView(name='Custom'))
    models = [User, Role, Post, Comment, Tag, Reminder]

    for model in models:
        admin.add_view(
            CustomModelView(model, db.session,
            category='models')
        )
```

The `category` keyword tells Flask Admin to put all of the views with the same category value into the same dropdown on the navigation bar.

If you go to the browser now, you will see a new drop-down menu labeled **Models** with links to the admin pages of all of the tables in the database as follows:

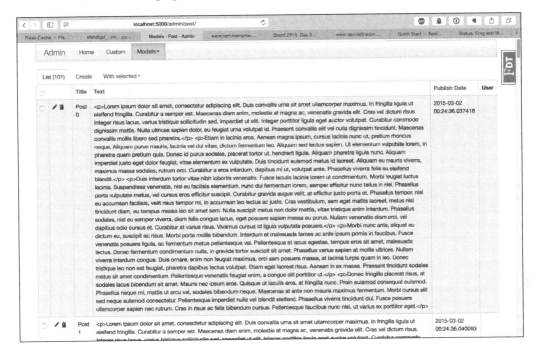

The generated interface for each model provides a lot of functionality. New posts can be created, and the existing posts can be deleted in bulk. All of the fields can be set from this interface, including the relationship fields, which are implemented as searchable drop-down menus. The date and datetime fields even have custom JavaScript inputs with calendar dropdowns. Overall, this is a huge improvement to the hand-created interface that was created in *Chapter 6, Securing Your App*.

Enhancing the post's administration

While this interface is a huge step-up in quality, there are some features missing. We no longer have the WYSIWYG editor that was available in the original interface, and this page can be improved by enabling some of the more powerful Flask Admin features.

To add the WYSIWYG editor back into the post creation page, we will need a new WTForms field, as Flask Admin constructs its forms with Flask WTF. We will also need to override the textarea field in the post edit and creation page with this new field type. The first thing that needs to be done is to create the new field type in forms.py by using the textarea field as a base:

```python
from wtforms import (
    widgets,
    StringField,
    TextAreaField,
    PasswordField,
    BooleanField
)

class CKTextAreaWidget(widgets.TextArea):
    def __call__(self, field, **kwargs):
        kwargs.setdefault('class_', 'ckeditor')
        return super(CKTextAreaWidget, self).__call__(field,
        **kwargs)

class CKTextAreaField(TextAreaField):
    widget = CKTextAreaWidget()
```

In this code, we created a new field type CKTextAreaField that adds a widget to the textarea, and all that the widget does is adds a class to the HTML tag. Now, to add this field to the Post admin page, the Post will need its own ModelView:

```python
from webapp.forms import CKTextAreaField

class PostView(CustomModelView):
    form_overrides = dict(text=CKTextAreaField)
    column_searchable_list = ('text', 'title')
    column_filters = ('publish_date',)

    create_template = 'admin/post_edit.html'
    edit_template = 'admin/post_edit.html'
```

There are several new things in this code. First, the `form_overrides` class variable tells Flask Admin to override the field type of the name text with this new field type. The `column_searchable_list` function defines which columns are searchable via text. Adding this will allow Flask Admin to include a search field on the overview page that searches the values of the defined fields. Next, the `column_filters` class variable tells Flask Admin to create a `filters` interface on the overview page of this model. The `filters` interface allows columns that are not text to be filtered down by adding conditions to the shown rows. An example with the preceding code is to create a filter that shows all rows with `publish_date` values greater than January 1, 2015. Finally, the `create_template` and `edit_template` class variables allow you to define custom templates for Flask Admin to use. For the custom template that we will be using, we need to create a new file `post_edit.html` in the admin folder. In this template, we will include the same JavaScript library that was used in *Chapter 6, Securing Your App*:

```
{% extends 'admin/model/edit.html' %}
{% block tail %}
    {{ super() }}
    <script
        src="//cdn.ckeditor.com/4.4.7/standard/ckeditor.js">
    </script>
{% endblock %}
```

The tail block of the inherited template is located at the end of the file. Once the template is created, your `post` edit and creation page should look like this:

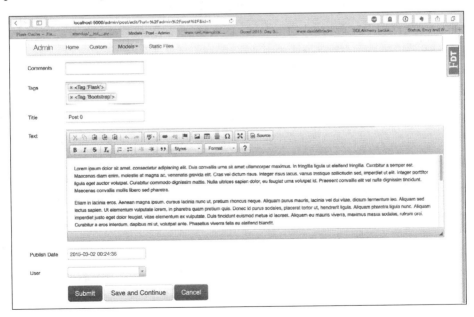

Creating file system admin pages

Another common function that most `admin` interfaces cover is being able to access the server's file system from the web. Thankfully, Flask Admin includes this feature with the `FileAdmin` class

```
class CustomFileAdmin(FileAdmin):
    pass
```

Now, just import the new class into your `__init__.py` file and pass in the path that you wish to be accessible from the web:

```
import os
from controllers.admin import (
    CustomView,
    CustomModelView,
    PostView,
    CustomFileAdmin
)


def create_app(object_name):

    admin.add_view(
        CustomFileAdmin(
            os.path.join(os.path.dirname(__file__), 'static'),
            '/static/',
            name='Static Files'
        )
    )
```

Securing Flask Admin

Currently, the entire `admin` interface is accessible to the world; let's fix that. The routes in the `CustomView` can be secured just like any other route:

```
class CustomView(BaseView):
    @expose('/')
    @login_required
    @admin_permission.require(http_exception=403)
    def index(self):
        return self.render('admin/custom.html')

    @expose('/second_page')
    @login_required
```

```
    @admin_permission.require(http_exception=403)
    def second_page(self):
        return self.render('admin/second_page.html')
```

To secure the `ModeView` and `FileAdmin` subclasses, they need to have a method named `is_accessible` defined, which either returns *true* or *false*.

```
class CustomModelView(ModelView):
    def is_accessible(self):
        return current_user.is_authenticated() and\
               admin_permission.can()

class CustomFileAdmin(FileAdmin):
    def is_accessible(self):
        return current_user.is_authenticated() and\
               admin_permission.can()
```

Because we set up our authentication correctly in *Chapter 6, Securing Your App*, this task was trivial.

Flask Mail

The final Flask extension that this chapter will cover is Flask Mail, which allows you to connect and configure your SMTP client from Flask's configuration. Flask Mail will also help to simplify application testing in *Chapter 12, Testing Flask Apps*. The first step is to install Flask Mail with `pip`:

$ pip install Flask-Mail

Next, the `Mail` object needs to be initialized in the `extentions.py` file:

```
from flask_mail import Mail

mail = Mail()
```

`flask_mail` will connect to our SMTP server of choice by reading the configuration variables in our `app` object, so we need to add those values to our `config` object:

```
class DevConfig(Config):

    MAIL_SERVER = 'localhost'
    MAIL_PORT = 25
    MAIL_USERNAME = 'username'
    MAIL_PASSWORD = 'password'
```

Finally, the `mail` object is initialized on the `app` object in `__init__.py`:

```
from .extensions import (
    bcrypt,
    oid,
    login_manager,
    principals,
    rest_api,
    celery,
    debug_toolbar,
    cache,
    assets_env,
    main_js,
    main_css,
    admin,
    mail
)


def create_app(object_name):

    mail.init_app(app)
```

To see how Flask Mail can simplify our e-mailing code, this is the remind task created in *Chapter 9, Creating Asynchronous Tasks with Celery*, but using Flask Mail instead of the standard library SMTP module:

```
from flask_mail import Message
from webapp.extensions import celery, mail

@celery.task(
    bind=True,
    ignore_result=True,
    default_retry_delay=300,
    max_retries=5
)
def remind(self, pk):
    reminder = Reminder.query.get(pk)
    msg = MIMEText(reminder.text)
    msg = Message("Your reminder",
                    sender="from@example.com",
                    recipients=[reminder.email])

    msg.body = reminder.text
    mail.send(msg)
```

Summary

This chapter has created a large increase in the functionality of our app. We now have a fully featured administrator interface, a useful debugging tool in the browser, two tools that greatly speed up page load times, and a utility to make sending e-mails less of a headache.

As was stated at the start of this chapter, Flask is bare-bones and allows you to pick and choose the functionality that you want. Therefore, it is important to keep in mind that it is not necessary to include all of these extensions in you app. If you are the only content creator of your app, maybe the command-line interface is all you need because adding in these features takes development time and maintenance time when they inevitably break. This warning is given at the end of the chapter because one of the main reasons many Flask apps become unwieldy is because they include so many extensions that testing and maintaining all of them becomes a very large task.

In the next chapter, you will learn the internals of how an extension works and how to create your own extension.

11
Building Your Own Extension

From the first chapter of this book, we have been adding Flask extensions to our app in order to add new features and save us from spending lots of time to reinvent the wheel. Up to this point, it was unknown how these Flask extensions worked. In this chapter, we will create two simple Flask extensions in order to better understand Flask's internals and allow you to extend Flask with your own functionality.

Creating a YouTube Flask extension

To begin, the first extension we are going to create is a simple extension that allows embedding YouTube videos in Jinja templates with the following tag:

```
{{ youtube(video_id) }}
```

The `video_id` object is the code after the `v` in any YouTube URL. For example, in the URL `https://www.youtube.com/watch?v=_OB1gSz8sSM`, the `video_id` object would be `_OB1gSz8sSM`.

For now, the code for this extension will reside in `extensions.py`. However, this is only for development and debugging purposes. When the code is ready to be shared, it will be moved into its own project directory.

The first thing that any Flask extension needs is the object that will be initialized on the app. This object will handle adding its `Blueprint` object to the app and registering the `youtube` function on Jinja:

```python
from flask import Blueprint

class Youtube(object):
    def __init__(self, app=None, **kwargs):
        if app:
            self.init_app(app)
```

```
    def init_app(self, app):
        self.register_blueprint(app)

    def register_blueprint(self, app):
        module = Blueprint(
            "youtube",
            __name__,
            template_folder="templates"
        )
        app.register_blueprint(module)
        return module
```

So far, the only thing this code does is initialize an empty blueprint on the `app` object. The next piece of code needed is a representation of a video. The following will be a class that will handle the parameters from the Jinja function and render HTML to display in the template:

```
from flask import (
    flash,
    redirect,
    url_for,
    session,
    render_template,
    Blueprint,
    Markup
)

class Video(object):
    def __init__(self, video_id, cls="youtube"):
        self.video_id = video_id
        self.cls = cls

    def render(self, *args, **kwargs):
        return render_template(*args, **kwargs)

    @property
    def html(self):
        return Markup(
            self.render('youtube/video.html', video=self)
        )
```

This object will be created from the `youtube` function in the template, and any arguments passed in the template will be given to this object to render HTML. There is also a new object in this code, `Markup`, which we never used before. The `Markup` class is Flask's way of automatically escaping HTML or marking it as safe to include in the template. If we just returned HTML, Jinja would autoescape it because it does not know whether it is safe or not. This is Flask's way of protecting your site from **cross-site scripting attacks**.

The next step is to create the function that will be registered in Jinja:

```
def youtube(*args, **kwargs):
    video = Video(*args, **kwargs)
    return video.html
```

In the `YouTube` class, we have to register the function to Jinja in the `init_app` method:

```
class Youtube(object):
    def __init__(self, app=None, **kwargs):
        if app:
            self.init_app(app)

    def init_app(self, app):
        self.register_blueprint(app)
        app.add_template_global(youtube)
```

Finally, we have to create HTML that will add the video to the page. In a new folder named `youtube` in the `templates` directory, create a new HTML file named `video.html` and add the following code to it:

```
<iframe
    class="{{ video.cls }}"
    width="560"
    height="315"
    src="https://www.youtube.com/embed/{{ video.video_id }}"
    frameborder="0"
    allowfullscreen>
</iframe>
```

This is all the code that's needed to embed YouTube videos in your templates. Let's test this out now. In `extensions.py`, initialize the `Youtube` class below the `Youtube` class definition:

```
youtube_ext = Youtube()
```

In `__init__.py`, import the `youtube_ext` variable and use the `init_app` method we created to register it on the app:

```
from .extensions import (
    bcrypt,
    oid,
    login_manager,
    principals,
    rest_api,
```

```
            celery,
            debug_toolbar,
            cache,
            assets_env,
            main_js,
            main_css,
            admin,
            mail,
            youtube_ext
    )

    def create_app(object_name):
        ...
        youtube_ext.init_app(app)
```

Now, as a simple example, add the `youtube` function to the top of the blog home page:

```
{{ youtube("_OB1gSz8sSM") }}
```

This will have the following result:

Creating a Python package

In order to make our new Flask extension available to others, we have to create an installable Python package from the code we have written so far. To begin, we need a new project directory outside our current application directory. We will need two things: a setup.py file, which we will fill in later, and a folder named flask_youtube. In the flask_youtube directory, we will have an __init__.py file, which will contain all the code that we wrote for our extension.

Here is the final version of that code contained in the __init__.py file:

```python
from flask import render_template, Blueprint, Markup

class Video(object):
    def __init__(self, video_id, cls="youtube"):
        self.video_id = video_id
        self.cls = cls

    def render(self, *args, **kwargs):
        return render_template(*args, **kwargs)

    @property
    def html(self):
        return Markup(
            self.render('youtube/video.html', video=self)
        )

def youtube(*args, **kwargs):
    video = Video(*args, **kwargs)
    return video.html

class Youtube(object):
    def __init__(self, app=None, **kwargs):
        if app:
            self.init_app(app)

    def init_app(self, app):
        self.register_blueprint(app)
        app.add_template_global(youtube)

    def register_blueprint(self, app):
        module = Blueprint(
            "youtube",
            __name__,
            template_folder="templates"
        )
        app.register_blueprint(module)
        return module
```

Also inside the `flask_youtube` directory, we will need a `templates` directory, which will hold the `youtube` directory that we put in our app's `templates` directory.

In order to turn this code into a Python package, we will use the library named `setuptools`. `setuptools` is a Python package that allows developers to easily create installable packages for their code. `setuptools` will bundle code so that `pip` and `easy_install` can automatically install them, and will even upload your package to the **Python Package Index (PyPI)**.

 All the packages that we have been installing from `pip` have come from PyPI. To see all the available packages, go to `https://pypi.python.org/pypi`.

All that is needed to get this functionality is to fill out the `setup.py` file:

```
from setuptools import setup, find_packages
setup(
    name='Flask-YouTube',
    version='0.1',
    license='MIT',
    description='Flask extension to allow easy embedding of YouTube
videos',
    author='Jack Stouffer',
    author_email='example@gmail.com',
    platforms='any',
    install_requires=['Flask'],
    packages=find_packages()
)
```

This code uses the `setup` function from `setuptools` to find your source code and make sure that the machine that is installing your code has the required packages. Most of the attributes are rather self-explanatory, except the package attribute, which uses the `find_packages` function from `setuptools`. What the `package` attribute does is it finds which parts of our source code are part of the package to be released. We use the `find_packages` method to automatically find which parts of the code to include. This is based on some sane defaults, such as looking for directories with `__init__.py` files and excluding common file extensions.

Although it is not mandatory, this setup also contains metadata about the author and the license, which would be included on the PyPI page if we were to upload this there. There is a lot more customization available in the `setup` function, so I encourage you to read the documentation at `http://pythonhosted.org/setuptools/`.

You can now install this package on your machine by running the following commands:

```
$ python setup.py build
$ python setup.py install
```

This will install your code into your Python `packages` directory, or if you're using `virtualenv`, it will install it to the local `packages` directory. Then, you can import your place on package via:

```
from flask_youtube import Youtube
```

Modifying the response with Flask extensions

So, we have created an extension that adds new functionality to our templates. But how would we create an extension which modifies the behavior of our app at the request level? To demonstrate this, let's create an extension that modifies all the responses from Flask by compressing the contents of the response. This is a common practice in web development in order to speed up page load times, as compressing objects with a method like **gzip** is very fast and relatively cheap CPU-wise. Normally, this would be handled at the server level. So, unless you wish to host your app with only Python code, which is possible and will be covered in *Chapter 13, Deploying Flask Apps*, this extension really doesn't have much use in the real world.

To achieve this, we will use the `gzip` module in the Python standard library to compress the contents after each request is processed. We will also have to add special HTTP headers into the response in order for the browser to know that the content is compressed. We will also need to check in the HTTP request headers whether the browser can accept gzipped contents.

Just as before, our content will initially reside in the `extensions.py` file:

```
from flask import request
from gzip import GzipFile
from io import BytesIO
...

class GZip(object):
    def __init__(self, app=None):
        self.app = app
        if app is not None:
            self.init_app(app)
```

```
        def init_app(self, app):
            app.after_request(self.after_request)

        def after_request(self, response):
            encoding = request.headers.get('Accept-Encoding', '')

            if 'gzip' not in encoding or \
                not response.status_code in (200, 201):
                return response

            response.direct_passthrough = False

            contents = BytesIO()
            with GzipFile(
                mode='wb',
                compresslevel=5,
                fileobj=contents) as gzip_file:
                gzip_file.write(response.get_data())

            response.set_data(bytes(contents.getvalue()))

            response.headers['Content-Encoding'] = 'gzip'
            response.headers['Content-Length'] = response.content_length

            return response

    flask_gzip = GZip()
```

Just as with the previous extension, our initializer for the compress object accommodates both the normal Flask setup and the application factory setup. In the `after_request` method, instead of registering a blueprint, we register a new function on the after-request event so that our extension can compress the results.

The `after_request` method is where the real logic of the extension comes into play. First, it checks whether the browser accepts gzip encoding by looking at the `Accept-Encoding` value in the request header. If the browser does not accept gzip, or did not return a successful response, the function just returns the contents and makes no modifications to it. However, if the browser does accept our content and the response was successful, then we will compress the content. We use another standard library class named `BytesIO`, which allows file streams to be written and stored in memory, and not in an intermediate file. This is necessary because the `GzipFile` object expects to write to a file object.

After the data is compressed, we set the response objects' data to the results of the compression and set the necessary HTTP header values in the response as well. Finally, the gzip contents are returned to the browser, and the browser then decompresses the contents, significantly speeding up the page load times.

In order to test the functionality in your browser, you have to disable **Flask Debug Toolbar**, because at the time of writing there is a bug in its code where it expects all responses to be encoded in UTF-8.

If you reload the page nothing should look different. However, if you use the developer tools in the browser of your choice and inspect the responses, you will see that they are compressed.

Summary

Now that we went through two different examples of different types of Flask extensions, you should have a very clear understanding of how most of the Flask extensions that we used work. Using the knowledge that you have now, you should be able to add any extra functionality to Flask that you need for your specific application.

In the next chapter, we are going to look at how to add testing to our application to take out the guesswork of whether changes we made to the code have broken any of the functionality of our application.

12
Testing Flask Apps

Throughout this book, every time that we have made a modification to our application's code, we have had to manually load the affected web pages into our browser to test if the code was working correctly. As the application grows, this process becomes more and more tedious, especially if you change something that is of low level and used everywhere, such as SQLAlchemy model code.

In order to automate the process of verifying that our code works the way we want it to, we will use a built-in feature of Python that allows us to write tests, normally named unit tests, which are checked against our application's code.

What are unit tests?

Testing a program is very simple. All it involves is running particular pieces of your program and saying what you expect the results to be and comparing it to what the results from the piece of the program actually are. If the results are the same, the test passes. If the results are different, the test fails. Typically, these tests are run before code is committed to the Git repository and before code is deployed to the live server in order to make sure that broken code doesn't make it into either of those systems.

In program testing, there are three main types of tests. Unit tests are tests that verify the correctness of individual pieces of code, such as functions. Second is integration testing, which tests the correctness of various units of programs working in tandem. The last type of testing is system testing, which tests the correctness of the whole system at once rather than in individual pieces.

In this chapter, we will be using unit testing and system testing in order to verify that our code is working as planned. We will not do integration testing in this chapter because the way in which various parts of the code work in tandem are not handled by the code we have written. For example, the way SQLAlchemy worked with Flask is not handled by our code. Flask SQLAlchemy handles it.

This brings us to one of the first rules of code testing. Write tests for code that you own. The first reason for this is it's very likely that a test for this could have already been written. The second reason is that any bugs in the libraries that you use will surface in your tests when you want to use that library's functionality.

How does testing work?

Let's start with a very simple Python function for us to test.

```
def square(x):
    return x * x
```

In order to verify the correctness of this code, we pass a value and we will test if the result of the function is what we expect. For example, we would give it an input of five and would expect the result to be 25.

To illustrate the concept, we can manually test this function in the command line using the `assert` statement. The `assert` statement in Python simply says that if the conditional statement after the `assert` keyword returns `False`, throw an exception as follows:

```
$ python
>>> def square(x):
...     return x * x
>>> assert square(5) == 25
>>> assert square(7) == 49
>>> assert square(10) == 100
>>> assert square(10) == 0
Traceback (most recent call last):
  File "<stdin>", line 1, in <module>
AssertionError
```

Using these `assert` statements, we verified that the square function was working as intended.

Unit testing the application

Unit testing in Python works by combining `assert` statements into their own functions inside a class. This collection of testing functions inside the class is called a test case. Each function inside the test case should test only one thing, which is the main idea behind unit testing. Testing only one thing in your unit tests forces you to verify each piece of code individually and not gloss over any of the functionality of your code. If you write your unit tests correctly, you will end up with lots and lots of them. While this may seem overly verbose, it will save you from headaches down the road.

Before we can build our test cases, we need another configuration object specifically to set up the app for testing. In this configuration, we will use the Python `tempfile` module in the standard library in order to create a test SQLite database in a file that will automatically delete itself when the tests are over. This allows us to guarantee that the tests will not interfere with our actual database. Also, the configuration disables WTForms CSRF checks to allow us to submit forms from the tests without the CSRF token.

```python
import tempfile

class TestConfig(Config):
    db_file = tempfile.NamedTemporaryFile()

    DEBUG = True
    DEBUG_TB_ENABLED = False

    SQLALCHEMY_DATABASE_URI = 'sqlite:///' + db_file.name

    CACHE_TYPE = 'null'
    WTF_CSRF_ENABLED = False

    CELERY_BROKER_URL = "amqp://guest:guest@localhost:5672//"
    CELERY_BACKEND_URL = "amqp://guest:guest@localhost:5672//"

    MAIL_SERVER = 'localhost'
    MAIL_PORT = 25
    MAIL_USERNAME = 'username'
    MAIL_PASSWORD = 'password'
```

Testing the route functions

Let's build our first test case. In this test case, we will be testing if the route functions successfully return a response if we access their URL. In a new directory at the root of the project directory named `tests`, create a new file named `test_urls.py`, which will hold all of the unit tests for the routes. Each test case should have its own file, and each test case should focus on one area of the code you are testing.

In `test_urls.py`, let's start creating what the built-in Python `unittest` library needs. The code will use the `unittest` library from Python in order to run all the tests that we create in the test case.

```python
import unittest

class TestURLs(unittest.TestCase):
    pass

if __name__ == '__main__':
    unittest.main()
```

Let's see what happens when this code is run. We will use the `unittest` library's ability to automatically find our test cases to run the tests. The pattern the `unittest` library looks for is `test*.py`:

```
$ python -m unittest discover


----------------------------------------------------------------------

Ran 0 tests in 0.000s


OK
```

Because there are no tests in the test case, the test case passed successfully.

 The test script was run from the parent directory of the script and not in the test folder itself. This is to allow imports of the application code inside the test scripts.

In order to test the URLs, we need to have a way to query the application's routes without actually running a server, so our requests are returned. Flask provides a way of accessing routes in tests named the test client. The test client gives methods to create HTTP requests on our routes without having to actually run the application with `app.run()`.

We will need the test client object for each of the tests in this test case, but adding in code in each unittest to create the test client doesn't make much sense when we have the setUp method. The setUp method is run before each unit test and can attach variables to self in order for the test method to have access to them. In our setUp method, we need to create the application object with our TestConfig object and create the test client.

Also, there are three bugs that we need to work around. The first two are in the Flask Admin and Flask Restful extensions, which do not remove the Blueprint objects stored internally when the application object they are applied to is destroyed. Third, Flask SQLAlchemy's initializer doesn't correctly add the application object while outside the webapp directory:

```
class TestURLs(unittest.TestCase):
    def setUp(self):
        # Bug workarounds
        admin._views = []
        rest_api.resources = []

        app = create_app('webapp.config.TestConfig')
        self.client = app.test_client()

        # Bug workaround
        db.app = app

        db.create_all()
```

All of the bugs previously listed exist at the time of writing and may no longer exist when you read this chapter.

Along with the setUp method, there is also the tearDown method, which is run every time a unit test ends. The tearDown method is to destroy any objects that were created in the setUp method that cannot be automatically garbage collected. In our case, we will use the tearDown method in order to delete the tables in the test database in order to have a clean slate for each test.

```
class TestURLs(unittest.TestCase):
    def setUp(self):
        ...

    def tearDown(self):
        db.session.remove()
        db.drop_all()
```

Now we can create our first unit test. The first test will test whether accessing the root of our application will return a `302 redirect` to the blog home page as follows:

```python
class TestURLs(unittest.TestCase):
    def setUp(self):
        ...

    def tearDown(self):
        ...

    def test_root_redirect(self):
        """ Tests if the root URL gives a 302 """

        result = self.client.get('/')
        assert result.status_code == 302
        assert "/blog/" in result.headers['Location']
```

Each unit test must start with the word `test` to tell the `unittest` library that the function is a unit test and not just some utility function inside the test case class.

Now if we run the tests again, we see our test being run and passing the checks:

```
$ python -m unittest discover
.
----------------------------------------------------------------
Ran 1 tests in 0.128s


OK
```

The best way to write tests is to ask yourself what you are looking for ahead of time, write the `assert` statements, and write the code needed to execute those asserts. This forces you to ask what you are really testing before you start writing the test. It's also the best practice to write a Python doc string for each unit test, as it will be printed with the name of the test whenever the test fails, and after you write 50+ tests, it can be helpful to know exactly what the test is for.

Rather than using the built-in `assert` keyword from Python, we can use some of the methods provided by the `unittest` library. These methods provide specialized error messages and debug information when the `assert` statements inside these functions fail.

The following is a list of all of the special `assert` statements given by the `unittest` library and what they do:

- `assertEqual(x, y)`: Assert x == y
- `assertNotEqual(x, y)`: Assert x != y
- `assertTrue(x)`: Assert x is True
- `assertFalse(x)`: Assert x is False
- `assertIs(x, y)`: Assert x is y
- `assertIsNot(x, y)`: Assert x is not y
- `assertIsNone(x)`: Assert x is None
- `assertIsNotNone(x)`: Assert x is not None
- `assertIn(x, y)`: Assert x in y
- `assertNotIn(x, y)`: Assert x not in y
- `assertIsInstance(x, y)`: Assert isinstance(x, y)
- `assertNotIsInstance(x, y)`: Assert not isinstance(x, y)

If we wanted to test the return value of a normal page, the unit test would look like this:

```
class TestURLs(unittest.TestCase):
    def setUp(self):
        ...

    def tearDown(self):
        ...

    def test_root_redirect(self):
        ...
```

Remember that this code is only testing if the URLs give returns successfully. The content of the return to data is not part of these tests.

If we wanted to test submitting a form like the login form, we can use the post method of the test client. Let's create a `test_login` method to see if the login form works correctly:

```
class TestURLs(unittest.TestCase):
    ...
    def test_login(self):
        """ Tests if the login form works correctly """

        test_role = Role("default")
        db.session.add(test_role)
        db.session.commit()

        test_user = User("test")
        test_user.set_password("test")
        db.session.add(test_user)
        db.session.commit()

        result = self.client.post('/login', data=dict(
            username='test',
            password="test"
        ), follow_redirects=True)

        self.assertEqual(result.status_code, 200)
        self.assertIn('You have been logged in', result.data)
```

The additional check for the string in the return data exists because the return code is not affected by the validity of the entered data. The post method will work for testing any of the form objects we have created throughout the book.

Now that you understand the mechanics of unit testing, you can use unit testing in order to test all the parts of your application. For example, testing all the routes in the application, testing any utility function that we have made like `sidebar_data`, testing if users with certain permissions can or cannot access a page, and so on.

If your application's code has a feature, no matter how small, you should have a test for it. Why? Because whatever can go wrong, will go wrong. If the validity of your application's code relies entirely on manual testing, then something is going to get overlooked as your app grows. When something gets overlooked, then broken code is deployed to live servers, which annoys your users.

User interface testing

In order to test the high level of our application's code, and to create system tests, we will write tests that work with browsers and verify that the UI code is functioning properly. Using a tool called Selenium, we will create Python code that hooks into a browser and controls it purely from code. You find elements on the screen and then perform actions on those elements by having Selenium. Click on it or input keystrokes. Also, Selenium allows you to perform checks on the page content by giving you access to the elements' content, such as its attributes and its inner text. For more advanced checks, Selenium even gives an interface to run arbitrary JavaScript on the page. If the JavaScript returns a value, it is automatically converted into a Python type.

Before we touch the code, Selenium needs to be installed:

```
$ pip install selenium
```

To begin with the code, our UI tests need a file of their own in the tests directory named `test_ui.py`. Because system tests do not test one specific thing, the best way to write user interface tests is to think of the test as going through a typical user's flow. Before you write the test, write down specific steps that our fake user is going to simulate:

```
import unittest

class TestURLs(unittest.TestCase):
    def setUp(self):
        pass

    def tearDown(self):
        pass

    def test_add_new_post(self):
        """ Tests if the new post page saves a Post object to the
            database

            1. Log the user in
            2. Go to the new_post page
            3. Fill out the fields and submit the form
            4. Go to the blog home page and verify that the post
               is on the page
        """
        pass
```

Now that we know exactly what our test is going to do, let's start adding in Selenium code. In the `setUp` and `tearDown` methods, we need code to start up a web browser that Selenium controls and then close it when the test is over.

```
import unittest
from selenium import webdriver
class TestURLs(unittest.TestCase):
    def setUp(self):
        self.driver = webdriver.Firefox()
    def tearDown(self):
        self.driver.close()
```

This code spawns a new Firefox window with Selenium controlling it. For this to work of course, you need Firefox installed on your computer. There is support for other browsers, but they all require an extra program for them to work correctly. Firefox has the best support out of all of the browsers.

Before we write the code for the test, let's explore the Selenium API as follows:

```
$ python
>>> from selenium import webdriver
>>> driver = webdriver.Firefox()
# load the Google homepage
>>> driver.get("http://www.google.com")
# find a element by its class
>>> search_field = driver.find_element_by_class_name("gsfi")
# find a element by its name
>>> search_field = driver.find_element_by_name("q")
# find an element by its id
>>> search_field = driver.find_element_by_id("lst-ib")
# find an element with JavaScript
>>> search_field = driver.execute_script(
    "return document.querySelector('#lst-ib')"
)
# search for flask
>>> search_field.send_keys("flask")
>>> search_button = driver.find_element_by_name("btnK")
>>> search_button.click()
```

These are the main functions from Selenium that we will be using, but there are many other ways to find and interact with elements on the web page. For the full list of available features, refer to the Selenium-Python documentation at `http://selenium-python.readthedocs.org`.

There are two gotchas in Selenium that need to be kept in mind while writing your tests, or you will run into very odd bugs that are almost impossible to debug from their error messages:

1. Selenium is designed to work like there is an actual person controlling the browser. This means that if an element cannot be seen on the page, Selenium cannot interact with it. For example, if an element covers another element you wish to click, say a modal window is in front of a button, then the button cannot be pushed. If the element's CSS has its display set to `none` or visibility set to `hidden`, the results will be the same.

2. All of the variables that point toward elements on the screen are stored as pointers to those elements in the browser, which means that they are not stored in Python's memory. If the page changes without using the `get` method, like when a link is clicked and a new element pointer is created, then the test will crash. This happens because the driver will be continuously looking for the elements on the previous page and not finding them on the new one. The `get` method of the driver clears out all those references.

In the previous tests, we used the test client in order to simulate a request to the application object. However, because we are now using something that needs to directly interface with the application through a web browser, we need an actual server to be running. This server needs to be run in a separate terminal window before the user interface tests are run so that they have something to request. To do this, we need a separate Python file in order to run the server with our test configuration, as well as setting up some models for our UI tests to use. In a new file at the root of the project directory named `run_test_server.py`, add the following:

```python
from webapp import create_app
from webapp.models import db, User, Role

app = create_app('webapp.config.TestConfig')

db.app = app
db.create_all()
```

```
default = Role("default")
poster = Role("poster")
db.session.add(default)
db.session.add(poster)
db.session.commit()

test_user = User("test")
test_user.set_password("test")
test_user.roles.append(poster)
db.session.add(test_user)
db.session.commit()

app.run()
```

Now that we have both the test server script and the knowledge of Selenium's API, we can finally write the code for our test:

```
class TestURLs(unittest.TestCase):
    def setUp(self):
        ...

    def tearDown(self):
        ...

    def test_add_new_post(self):
        """ Tests if the new post page saves a Post object to the
            database

            1. Log the user in
            2. Go to the new_post page
            3. Fill out the fields and submit the form
            4. Go to the blog home page and verify that
                the post is on the page
        """
        # login
        self.driver.get("http://localhost:5000/login")

        username_field = self.driver.find_element_by_name(
            "username"
        )
        username_field.send_keys("test")
```

```
password_field = self.driver.find_element_by_name(
    "password"
)
password_field.send_keys("test")

login_button = self.driver.find_element_by_id(
    "login_button"
)
login_button.click()

# fill out the form
self.driver.get("http://localhost:5000/blog/new")

title_field = self.driver.find_element_by_name("title")
title_field.send_keys("Test Title")

# find the editor in the iframe
self.driver.switch_to.frame(
    self.driver.find_element_by_tag_name("iframe")
)
post_field = self.driver.find_element_by_class_name(
    "cke_editable"
)
post_field.send_keys("Test content")
self.driver.switch_to.parent_frame()

post_button = self.driver.find_element_by_class_name(
    "btn-primary"
)
post_button.click()

# verify the post was created
self.driver.get("http://localhost:5000/blog")
self.assertIn("Test Title", self.driver.page_source)
self.assertIn("Test content", self.driver.page_source)
```

Most of this test uses the methods that we introduced earlier. However, there is a new method in this test named `switch_to`. The `switch_to` method is the context of the driver to allow the selection of elements inside an `iframe` element. Normally, it's impossible for the parent window to select any elements inside an `iframe` using JavaScript, but because we are directly interfacing into the browser itself, we can access `iframe` element's contents. We need to switch contacts like these because the WYSIWYG editor inside the post creation page uses `iframe` in order to create itself. After we are done with selecting elements within the `iframe`, we need to switch back to the parent context with the `parent_frame` method.

You now have the tools that you need to test both your server code and your user interface code completely. For the rest of the chapter, we will focus on tools and methodologies in order to make your testing even more effective in ensuring your application's correctness.

Test coverage

Now that our tests have been written, we have to know whether our code is sufficiently tested. The concept of test coverage, also known as code coverage, was invented to solve this issue. In any project, the test coverage represents what percentage of the code in the project was executed when the tests were run, and which lines were never run. This gives an idea of what parts of the project aren't being tested in our unit tests. To add coverage reports to our project, install the coverage library with pip as follows:

```
$ pip install coverage
```

The coverage library can be run as a command-line program that will run your test suite and take its measurements while the tests are running.

```
$ coverage run --source webapp --branch -m unittest discover
```

The `--source` flag tells coverage to only report on the coverage for the files in the `webapp` directory. If that weren't included, the percentages for all the libraries used in the app would be included as well. By default, if any code in an `if` statement is executed, the entire `if` statement is said to have executed. The `--branch` flag tells `coverage` to disable this and measure everything.

After `coverage` runs our tests and takes its measurements, we can see a report of its findings in two ways. The first is to see a print out of each file's coverage percentage on the command line:

```
$ coverage report
```

Name	Stmts	Miss	Branch	BrMiss	Cover
webapp/__init__	51	0	6	0	100%
webapp/config	37	0	0	0	100%
webapp/controllers/__init__	0	0	0	0	100%
webapp/controllers/admin	27	4	0	0	85%
webapp/controllers/blog	77	45	8	8	38%
webapp/controllers/main	78	42	20	16	41%
webapp/controllers/rest/__init__	0	0	0	0	100%
webapp/controllers/rest/auth	13	6	2	2	47%
webapp/controllers/rest/fields	17	8	0	0	53%
webapp/controllers/rest/parsers	19	0	0	0	100%
webapp/controllers/rest/post	85	71	44	43	12%
webapp/extensions	56	14	4	4	70%
webapp/forms	48	15	10	7	62%
webapp/models	89	21	4	3	74%
webapp/tasks	41	29	4	4	27%
TOTAL	638	255	102	87	54%

The second is to use coverage's HTML generating ability to see a detailed breakdown of each file in the browser.

```
$ coverage html
```

The preceding command creates a directory named `htmlcov`. When the `index.html` file is opened in the browser, each file name can be clicked on to reveal the breakdown of what lines were and were not run during the tests.

```
43              recent=recent,
44              top_tags=top_tags
45          )
46
47
48  @blog_blueprint.route('/post/<int:post_id>', methods=('GET', 'POST'))
49  @cache.cached(timeout=60)
50  def post(post_id):
51      form = CommentForm()
52
53      if form.validate_on_submit():
54          new_comment = Comment()
55          new_comment.name = form.name.data
56          new_comment.text = form.text.data
57          new_comment.post_id = post_id
58          new_comment.date = datetime.datetime.now()
59
60          db.session.add(new_comment)
61          db.session.commit()
62
63      post = Post.query.get_or_404(post_id)
64      tags = post.tags
65      comments = post.comments.order_by(Comment.date.desc()).all()
66      recent, top_tags = sidebar_data()
67
68      return render_template(
69          'post.html',
70          post=post,
71          tags=tags,
72          comments=comments,
73          recent=recent,
74          top_tags=top_tags,
75          form=form
76      )
77
78
79  @blog_blueprint.route('/new', methods=['GET', 'POST'])
80  @login_required
81  @poster_permission.require(http_exception=403)
82  def new_post():
83      form = PostForm()
84
85      if form.validate_on_submit():
86          new_post = Post(form.title.data)
```

In the preceding screenshot, the `blog.py` file was opened, and the coverage report clearly shows that the post route was never executed. However, this also gives some false negatives. As the user interface tests are not testing code that is being run by the coverage program, it doesn't count toward our coverage report. In order to fix this, just to make sure that you have tests in your test cases, test each individual function that would have been tested in the user interface tests.

In most projects, the percentage to aim for is around 90% code coverage. It's very rare that a project will have 100% of its code testable, and this possibility decreases as the size of the project increases.

Test-driven development

Now that we have our tests written, how can they be integrated into the development process? Currently, we are using our tests in order to ensure code correctness after we create some feature. But, what if we flipped the order and used tests in order to create correct code from the beginning? This is what **test-driven development (TDD)** advocates.

TDD follows a simple loop to write the code of a new feature in your application:

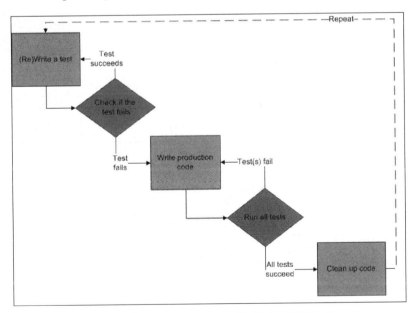

Credit for this image goes to user Excirial on Wikipedia

In a project that uses TDD, the first thing that you write, before any of the code that controls what you are actually building, is the tests. What this forces the programmers on the project to do is to plan out the project's scope, design, and requirements before writing any code. While designing APIs, it also forces the programmer to design the interface of the API from a consumer's perspective rather than design the interface after all the backend code has been written.

In TDD, tests are designed to fail the first time that you run them. There is a saying in TDD that if your tests don't fail the first time that you run them, you're not really testing anything. What this means is that you are most likely testing to what the tested unit gives rather than what it should give while writing tests after the fact.

After your tests fail the first time, you continuously write code until all the tests pass. This process is repeated for each new feature.

Once all of the original tests pass and the code is cleaned up, TDD tells you to stop writing code. By only writing code until the tests pass, TDD also enforces the **You Aren't Going To Need It** (**YAGNI**) philosophy, which states that programmers should only implement what they actually need rather than what they perceive they will need. A huge amount of wasted effort is made during development when programmers try to preemptively add functionality when no one needed it.

For example, on a PHP project that I worked on, I found the following code that looked for images in a directory:

```
$images = glob(
    $img_directory . "{*.jpg, *.jpeg, *.gif, *.png, *.PNG, *.Png,
*.PnG, *.pNG, *.pnG, *.pNg, *.PNg}",
    GLOB_BRACE
);
```

In PHP, glob is a function that looks through the contents of a directory to find files that match the pattern. I confronted the programmer who wrote it. His explanation for all the different versions of the .png extension was that some user uploaded a file with a .PNG extension, and the function didn't find it because it was only looking for the lowercase versions of the extensions. Instead of adding the uppercase versions to fix the problem at hand, he tried to fix a problem that didn't exist to make sure that he didn't have to touch this code again. We may feel like wasting a small amount of time, but this code was a microcosm of the entire code base. If this project followed TDD, a test case would have been added for the uppercase file extensions, the code added to pass the test, and that would have been the end of it.

TDD also promotes the idea of **Keep It Simple, Stupid (KISS)**, which dictates that simplicity should be a design goal from the beginning. TDD promotes KISS because it requires small, testable units of code that can be separated from each other and don't rely on a shared global state.

Also, in projects that follow TDD, there is an always-current documentation through the tests. One of the axioms of programming is that with any sufficiently large program, the documentation will always be out of date. This is because the documentation is one of the last things on the mind of the programmer when he/she is changing the code. However, with tests there are clear examples of each piece of functionality in the project (if the project has a large code coverage percentage). The tests are updated all the time and therefore show good examples of how the functions and API of the program should work.

Now that you understand Flask's functionality and how to write tests for Flask, the next project that you create in Flask can be entirely made with TDD.

Summary

Now that you understand testing and what it can do for your application, you can create applications that are guaranteed to be less bug-ridden. You will spend less time fixing bugs and more time adding features that are requested by your users.

In the next chapter, we will finish the book by going over ways to deploy your application into a production environment on a server.

As a final challenge to the reader, before moving onto the next chapter try to get your code coverage over 95%.

13
Deploying Flask Apps

Now that we have reached the last chapter of the book and have a fully functioning web app made in Flask, the final step to take in our development is to make the app available for the world. There are many different approaches to host your Flask app, each of them with their own pros and cons. This chapter will cover the best solutions and guide you in what situations you should choose one over the other.

Note that, in this chapter, the term server is used to refer to the physical machine that is running the operating system. But, when the term web server is used, it refers to the program on the server that receives HTTP requests and sends responses.

Deploying on your own server

The most common way to deploy any web app is to run it on a server that you have control over. In this case, control means access to a terminal on the server with an administrator account. This type of deployment gives you the most amount of freedom out of the other choices as it allows you to install any program or tool you wish. This is in contrast to other hosting solutions where the web server and database are chosen for you. This type of deployment also happens to be the least expensive option.

The downside to this freedom is that you take the responsibility of keeping the server up, backing up user data, keeping the software on the server up to date to avoid security issues, and so on. All books have been written on good server management. So if this is not a responsibility that you believe you or your company can handle, it would be best if you choose one of the other deployment options.

This section will be based on a Debian Linux-based server, as Linux is far and away the most popular OS to run web servers and Debian is the most popular Linux distro (a particular combination of software and the Linux kernel released as a package). Any OS with bash and a program named SSH (which will be introduced in the next section) will work for this chapter. The only differences will be the command-line programs to install software on the server.

Each of these web servers will use a protocol named **Web Server Gateway Interface** (**WSGI**), which is a standard designed to allow Python web applications to easily communicate with web servers. We will never directly work with WSGI, but most of the web server interfaces we will be using will have WSGI in their name and it can be confusing if you don't know what it is.

Pushing code to your server with fabric

To automate the process of setting up and pushing our application code to the server, we will use a Python tool named fabric. Fabric is a command-line program that reads and executes Python scripts on remote servers using a tool named SSH. SSH is a protocol that allows a user of one computer to remotely log in to another computer and execute commands on the command line, provided that the user has an account on the remote machine.

To install `fabric`, we will use `pip` as follows:

```
$ pip install fabric
```

`fabric` commands are collections of command-line programs to be run on the remote machine's shell, in this case, bash. We are going to make three different commands: one to run our unit tests, one to set up a brand new server to our specifications, and one to have the server update its copy of the application code with `git`. We will store these commands in a new file at the root of our project directory named `fabfile.py`.

As it's the easiest to create, let's make the test command first:

```
from fabric.api import local

def test():
    local('python -m unittest discover')
```

To run this function from the command line, we can use `fabric` command-line interface by passing the name of the command to run:

```
$ fab test
[localhost] local: python -m unittest discover

.....

---------------------------------------------------------------

Ran 5 tests in 6.028s

OK
```

Fabric has three main commands: `local`, `run`, and `sudo`. The `local` function, as seen in the preceding function, `run` commands on the local computer. The `run` and `sudo` functions run commands on a remote machine, but `sudo` runs commands as an administrator. All of these functions notify fabric whether the command ran successfully or not. If the command didn't run successfully, which means that, in this case, our tests failed, any other commands in the function will not be run. This is useful for our commands because it allows us to force ourselves not to push any code to the server that does not pass our tests.

Now we need to create the command to set up a new server from scratch. What this command will do is install the software that our production environment needs as well as downloads the code from our centralized `git` repository. It will also create a new user that will act as the runner of the web server as well as the owner of the code repository.

 Do not run your web server or have your code deployed by the root user. This opens your application to a whole host of security vulnerabilities.

This command will differ based on your operating system, and we will be adding this command in the rest of the chapter based on what server you choose:

```python
from fabric.api import env, local, run, sudo, cd

env.hosts = ['deploy@[your IP]']

def upgrade_libs():
    sudo("apt-get update")
    sudo("apt-get upgrade")
```

```
def setup():
    test()
    upgrade_libs()

    # necessary to install many Python libraries
    sudo("apt-get install -y build-essential")
    sudo("apt-get install -y git")
    sudo("apt-get install -y python")
    sudo("apt-get install -y python-pip")
    # necessary to install many Python libraries
    sudo("apt-get install -y python-all-dev")

    run("useradd -d /home/deploy/ deploy")
    run("gpasswd -a deploy sudo")

    # allows Python packages to be installed by the deploy user
    sudo("chown -R deploy /usr/local/")
    sudo("chown -R deploy /usr/lib/python2.7/")

    run("git config --global credential.helper store")

    with cd("/home/deploy/"):
        run("git clone [your repo URL]")

    with cd('/home/deploy/webapp'):
        run("pip install -r requirements.txt")
        run("python manage.py createdb")
```

There are two new fabric features in this script. The first is the env.hosts assignment, which tells fabric the user and IP address of the machine it should be logging in to. Second, there is the cd function used in conjunction with the with keyword, which executes any functions in the context of that directory instead of the home directory of the deploy user. The line that modifies the git configuration is there to tell git to remember your repository's username and password, so you do not have to enter it every time you wish to push code to the server. Also, before the server is set up, we make sure to update the server's software to keep the server up to date.

Finally, we have the function to push our new code to the server. In time, this command will also restart the web server and reload any configuration files that come from our code. But that depends on the server you choose, so this is filled out in the subsequent sections.

```
def deploy():
    test()
    upgrade_libs()
    with cd('/home/deploy/webapp'):
        run("git pull")
        run("pip install -r requirements.txt")
```

So, if we were to begin working on a new server, all we would need to do to set it up is to run the following commands:

```
$ fabric setup
$ fabric deploy
```

Running your web server with supervisor

Now that we have automated our updating process, we need some program on the server to make sure that our web server, and database if you aren't using SQLite, is running. To do this, we will use a simple program called supervisor. All that supervisor does is automatically runs command-line programs in background processes and allows you to see the status of the running programs. Supervisor also monitors all of the processes it's running, and if the process dies, it tries to restart it.

To install supervisor, we need to add it to the setup command in our fabfile.py:

```
def setup():
    ...
    sudo("apt-get install -y supervisor")
```

To tell supervisor what to do, we need to create a configuration file and then copy it to the /etc/supervisor/conf.d/ directory of our server during the deploy fabric command. Supervisor will load all of the files in this directory when it starts and attempts to run them.

In a new file in the root of our project directory named `supervisor.conf`, add the following:

```
[program:webapp]
command=
directory=/home/deploy/webapp
user=deploy

[program:rabbitmq]
command=rabbitmq-server
user=deploy

[program:celery]
command=celery worker -A celery_runner
directory=/home/deploy/webapp
user=deploy
```

> This is the bare minimum configuration needed to get a web server up and running. But, supervisor has a lot more configuration options. To view all of the customizations, go to the supervisor documentation at http://supervisord.org/.

This configuration tells `supervisor` to run a command in the context of /home/deploy/webapp under the `deploy` user. The right hand of the command value is empty because it depends on what server you are running and will be filled in for each section.

Now we need to add a `sudo` call in the deploy command to copy this configuration file to the /etc/supervisor/conf.d/ directory as follows.

```
def deploy():
    ...
    with cd('/home/deploy/webapp'):
        ...
        sudo("cp supervisord.conf /etc/supervisor/conf.d/webapp.conf")

    sudo('service supervisor restart')
```

A lot of projects just create the files on the server and forget about them, but having the configuration file stored in our `git` repository and copied on every deployment gives several advantages. First, this means that it is easy to revert changes if something goes wrong using `git`. Second, it means that we don't have to log in to our server in order to make changes to the files.

 Don't use the Flask development server in production. It not only fails to handle concurrent connections but also allows arbitrary Python code to be run on your server.

Gevent

The simplest option to get a web server up and running is to use a Python library named gevent to host your application. Gevent is a Python library that adds an alternative way of doing concurrent programming outside the Python threading library called **co-routines**. Gevent has an interface to run WSGI applications that is both simple and has good performance. A simple gevent server can easily handle hundreds of concurrent users, which is 99% more than the users of websites on the Internet will ever have. The downside to this option is that its simplicity means a lack of configuration options. There is no way, for example, to add rate limiting to the server or to add HTTPS traffic. This deployment option is purely for sites that you don't expect to receive a huge amount of traffic. Remember YAGNI; only upgrade to a different web server if you really need to.

 Co-routines are a bit outside of the scope of this book, so a good explanation can be found at `https://en.wikipedia.org/wiki/Coroutine`.

To install gevent, we will use `pip`:

```
$ pip install gevent
```

In a new file in the root of the project directory named `gserver.py`, add the following:

```
from gevent.wsgi import WSGIServer
from webapp import create_app

app = create_app('webapp.config.ProdConfig')

server = WSGIServer(('', 80), app)
server.serve_forever()
```

To run the server with supervisor, just change the command value to the following:

```
[program:webapp]
command=python gserver.py
directory=/home/deploy/webapp
user=deploy
```

Now when you deploy, `gevent` will be automatically installed for you by running your `requirements.txt` on every deployment, that is, if you are properly pip freezing after every new dependency is added.

Tornado

Tornado is another very simple way to deploy WSGI apps purely with Python. Tornado is a web server that is designed to handle thousands of simultaneous connections. If your application needs real-time data, Tornado also supports WebSockets for continuous, long-lived connections to the server.

 Do not use Tornado in production on a Windows server. The Windows version of Tornado is not only much slower, but it is considered beta quality software.

To use Tornado with our application, we will use Tornado's `WSGIContainer` in order to wrap the application object to make it Tornado compatible. Then, Tornado will start to listen on port *80* for requests until the process is terminated. In a new file named `tserver.py`, add the following:

```
from tornado.wsgi import WSGIContainer
from tornado.httpserver import HTTPServer
from tornado.ioloop import IOLoop
from webapp import create_app
app = WSGIContainer(create_app("webapp.config.ProdConfig"))
http_server = HTTPServer(app)
http_server.listen(80)
IOLoop.instance().start()
```

To run the Tornado with supervisor, just change the command value to the following:

```
[program:webapp]
command=python tserver.py
directory=/home/deploy/webapp
user=deploy
```

Nginx and uWSGI

If you need more performance or customization, the most popular way to deploy a Python web application is to use the web server Nginx as a frontend for the WSGI server uWSGI by using a reverse proxy. A reverse proxy is a program in networks that retrieves contents for a client from a server as if they returned from the proxy itself:

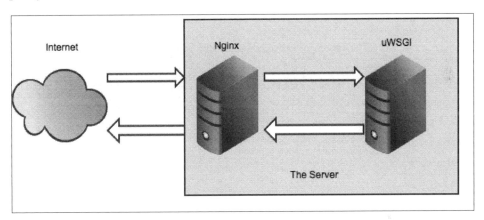

Nginx and uWSGI are used in this way because we get the power of the Nginx frontend while having the customization of uWSGI.

Nginx is a very powerful web server that became popular by providing the best combination of speed and customization. Nginx is consistently faster than other web severs such as Apache httpd and has native support for WSGI applications. The way it achieves this speed is several good architecture decisions as well as the decision early on that they were not going to try to cover a large amount of use cases like Apache does. Having a smaller feature set makes it much easier to maintain and optimize the code. From a programmer's perspective, it is also much easier to configure Nginx, as there is no giant default configuration file (`httpd.conf`) that needs to be overridden with `.htaccess` files in each of your project directories.

One downside is that Nginx has a much smaller community than Apache, so if you have an obscure problem, you are less likely to be able to find answers online. Also, it's possible that a feature that most programmers are used to in Apache isn't supported in Nginx.

uWSGI is a web server that supports several different types of server interfaces, including WSGI. uWSGI handles severing the application content as well as things such as load balancing traffic across several different processes and threads.

To install uWSGI, we will use `pip`:

```
$ pip install uwsgi
```

In order to run our application, uWSGI needs a file with an accessible WSGI application. In a new file named `wsgi.py` in the top level of the project directory, add the following:

```
from webapp import create_app

app = create_app("webapp.config.ProdConfig")
```

To test uWSGI, we can run it from the command line with the following:

```
$ uwsgi --socket 127.0.0.1:8080 \
--wsgi-file wsgi.py \
--callable app \
--processes 4 \
--threads 2
```

If you are running this on your server, you should be able to access port *8080* and see your app (if you don't have a firewall that is).

What this command does is load the app object from the `wsgi.py` file and makes it accessible from `localhost` on port *8080*. It also spawns four different processes with two threads each, which are automatically load balanced by a master process. This amount of processes is overkill for the vast, vast majority of websites. To start off, use a single process with two threads and scale up from there.

Instead of adding all of the configuration options on the command line, we can create a text file to hold our configuration, which brings the same benefits for configuration that were listed in the section on supervisor.

In a new file in the root of the project directory named `uwsgi.ini`, add the following code:

```
[uwsgi]
socket = 127.0.0.1:8080
wsgi-file = wsgi.py
callable = app
processes = 4
threads = 2
```

> uWSGI supports hundreds of configuration options as well as several official and unofficial plugins. To leverage the full power of uWSGI, you can explore the documentation at `http://uwsgi-docs.readthedocs.org/`.

Let's run the server now from supervisor:

```
[program:webapp]
command=uwsgi uwsgi.ini
directory=/home/deploy/webapp
user=deploy
```

We also need to install Nginx within the setup function:

```
def setup():
    ...
    sudo("apt-get install -y nginx")
```

Because we are installing Nginx from the OS's package manager, the OS will handle running of Nginx for us.

> At the time of writing, the Nginx version in the official Debian package manager is several years old. To install the most recent version, follow the instructions here: `http://wiki.nginx.org/Install`.

Next, we need to create an Nginx configuration file and then copy it to the `/etc/nginx/sites-available/` directory when we push the code. In a new file in the root of the project directory named `nginx.conf`, add the following:

```
server {
    listen 80;
    server_name your_domain_name;

    location / {
        include uwsgi_params;
        uwsgi_pass 127.0.0.1:8080;
    }

    location /static {
        alias /home/deploy/webapp/webapp/static;
    }
}
```

What this configuration file does is it tells Nginx to listen for incoming requests on port *80*, and forwards all requests to the WSGI application that is listening on port *8080*. Also, it makes an exception for any requests for static files and instead sends those requests directly to the file system. Bypassing uWSGI for static files gives a great performance boost, as Nginx is really good at serving static files quickly.

Finally, in the `fabfile.py` file:

```
def deploy():
    ...
    with cd('/home/deploy/webapp'):
        ...
        sudo("cp nginx.conf "
            "/etc/nginx/sites-available/[your_domain]")
        sudo("ln -sf /etc/nginx/sites-available/your_domain "
            "/etc/nginx/sites-enabled/[your_domain]")

    sudo("service nginx restart")
```

Apache and uWSGI

Using Apache httpd with uWSGI has mostly the same setup. First off, we need an apache configuration file in a new file in the root of our project directory named `apache.conf`:

```
<VirtualHost *:80>
    <Location />
        ProxyPass / uwsgi://127.0.0.1:8080/
    </Location>
</VirtualHost>
```

This file just tells Apache to pass all requests on port *80* to the uWSGI web server listening on port *8080*. However, this functionality requires an extra Apache plugin from uWSGI named `mod-proxy-uwsgi`. We can install this as well as Apache in the set command:

```
def setup():

    sudo("apt-get install -y apache2")
    sudo("apt-get install -y libapache2-mod-proxy-uwsgi")
```

Finally, in the `deploy` command, we need to copy our Apache configuration file into Apache's configuration directory:

```
def deploy():
    ...
    with cd('/home/deploy/webapp'):
        ...
        sudo("cp apache.conf "
            "/etc/apache2/sites-available/[your_domain]")
        sudo("ln -sf /etc/apache2/sites-available/[your_domain] "
            "/etc/apache2/sites-enabled/[your_domain]")

        sudo("service apache2 restart")
```

Deploying on Heroku

Heroku is the first of the **Platform as a Service (PaaS)** providers that this chapter will cover. PaaS is a service given to web developers that allows them to host their websites on a platform that is controlled and maintained by someone else. At the cost of freedom, you gain assurances that your website will automatically scale with the number of users your site has with no extra work on your part. Using PaaS also tends to be more expensive than running your own servers.

Heroku is PaaS that aims to be easy to use for web developers by hooking into already existing tools and not requiring any large changes in the app. Heroku works by reading the file named Procfile, which contains commands that your Heroku dyno basically a virtual machine sitting on a server, will run. Before we begin, you will need a Heroku account. If you wish to just experiment, there is a free account available.

In a new file named Procfile in the root of the directory, add the following:

```
web: uwsgi uwsgi.ini
```

This tells Heroku that we have a process named web, which will run the uWSGI command and pass the uwsgi.ini file. Heroku also needs a file named runtime. txt, which will tell it what Python runtime you wish to use, (at the time of writing, the latest Python release is 2.7.10):

```
python-2.7.10
```

Finally, we need to make some modifications to the uwsgi.ini file that we made earlier:

```
[uwsgi]
http-socket = :$(PORT)
die-on-term = true
wsgi-file = wsgi.py
callable = app
processes = 4
threads = 2
```

We set the port at uWSGI listens to the environment variable port because Heroku does not directly expose the dyno to the Internet. Instead, it has a very complicated load balancer and reverse proxy system, so we need to have uWSGI listen on the port that Heroku needs us to listen on. Also, we set **die-on-term** to true so that uWSGI listens for a signal termination event from the OS correctly.

To work with Heroku's command-line tools, we first need to install them, which can be done from `https://toolbelt.heroku.com`.

Next, you need to log in to your account:

```
$ heroku login
```

We can test our setup to make sure that it will work on Heroku before we deploy it by using the foreman command:

```
$ foreman start web
```

Foreman command simulates the same production environment that Heroku uses run our app. To create the dyno, which will run the application on Heroku's servers, we will use the `create` command. Then, we can push to the remote branch Heroku on our `git` repository to have Heroku servers automatically pull down our changes.

```
$ heroku create
$ git push heroku master
```

If everything went well, you should have a working application on your new Heroku dyno. You can open a new tab to your new web application with the following command:

```
$ heroku open
```

To see the app on a Heroku deployment in action, visit `https://mastering-flask.herokuapp.com/`.

Using Heroku Postgres

Maintaining a database properly is a full-time job. Thankfully, we can use one of Heroku's built-in features in order to automate this process for us. Heroku Postgres is a Postgres database that is maintained and hosted entirely by Heroku. Because we are using SQLAlchemy, using Heroku Postgres is trivial. In your dyno's dashboard, there is a link to your **Heroku Postgres** information. By clicking on it, you will be taken to a page as the one shown here:

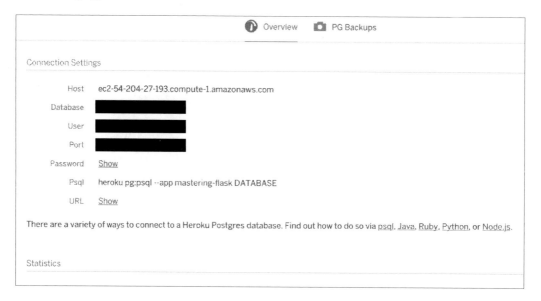

By clicking on the **URL** field, you will have an SQLAlchemy URL, which you can directly copy to your production configuration object.

Using Celery on Heroku

We have our production web server and database setup, but we still need to set up Celery. Using one of Heroku's many plugins, we can host a RabbitMQ instance in the cloud while running the Celery worker on the dyno.

The first step is to tell Heroku to run your celery worker in the `Procfile`:

```
web: uwsgi uwsgi.ini
celery: celery worker -A celery_runner
```

Next, to install the Heroku RabbitMQ plugin with the free plan (named the `lemur` plan), use the following command:

```
$ heroku addons:create cloudamqp:lemur
```

 To get the full list of Heroku add-ons, go to `https://elements.heroku.com/addons`.

At the same location on the dashboard where Heroku Postgres was listed, you will now find **CloudAMQP**:

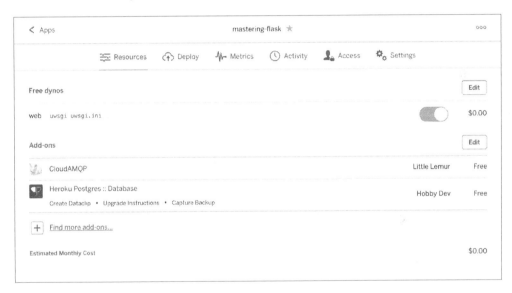

Clicking on it will also give you a screen with a copiable URL, which you can paste into your production configuration:

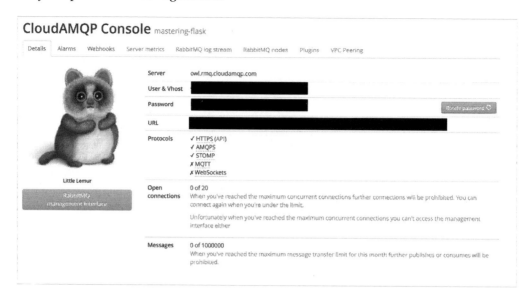

Deploying on Amazon web services

Amazon Web Services (AWS) is a collection of application platforms maintained by Amazon and built on top of the same infrastructure that runs `amazon.com`. To deploy our Flask code, we will be using Amazon Elastic Beanstalk, while the database will be hosted on Amazon Relational Database Service, and our messaging queue for Celery will be hosted on Amazon Simple Queue Service.

Using Flask on Amazon Elastic Beanstalk

Elastic Beanstalk is a platform for web applications that offers many powerful features for developers, so web developers do not have to worry about maintaining servers.

For example, your Elastic Beanstalk application will automatically scale by utilizing more and more servers as the number of people using your app at once grows. For Python apps, Elastic Beanstalk uses Apache in combination with `mod_wsgi` to connect to WSGI applications, so there is no extra configuration needed.

Before we begin, you will need an `Amazon.com` account and log in to `http://aws.amazon.com/elasticbeanstalk`. When you are logged in, you will see a screen like the following image:

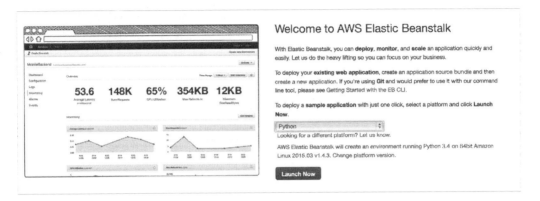

Click on the dropdown to select Python, and if your application needs a specific Python version, be sure to click on **Change platform version** and select the Python version you need. You will be taken through a setup process, and finally your app will go through an initialization process on Amazon's servers. While this is working, we can install the Elastic Beanstalk command-line tools. These tools will allow us to automatically deploy new versions of our application. To install them, use `pip`:

```
$ pip install awsebcli
```

Before we can deploy the application, you will need an AWS Id and access key. To do this, click on the dropdown that displays your username at the top of the page and click on **Security Credentials**.

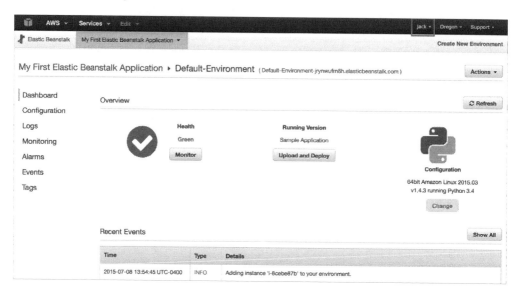

Then, click on the gray box that says **Access Keys** to get your ID and key pair:

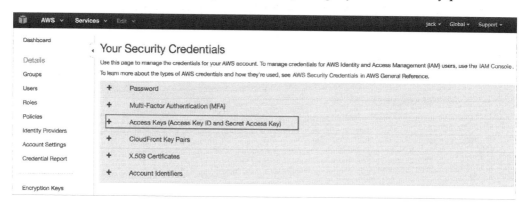

Once you have your key pair, do not share it with anyone because it will give anyone access to have a complete control over all of your platform instances on AWS. Now we can set up the command-line tools. In your project directory, run the following command:

```
$ eb init
```

Select the application that you created earlier to tie this directory to that application. We can see what is running on the application instance now by running the following:

```
$ eb open
```

Right now, you should just see a placeholder application. Let's change that by deploying our app. Elastic Beanstalk looks for a file named `application.py` in your project directory, and it expects a WSGI application named application in that file, so let's create that file now:

```
from webapp import create_app
application = create_app("webapp.config.ProdConfig")
```

Once that file is created, we can finally deploy the application:

```
$ eb deploy
```

This is needed to run Flask on AWS. To see the book's application running on Elastic Beanstalk, go to `http://masteringflask.elasticbeanstalk.com`.

Using Amazon Relational Database Service

Amazon Relational Database Service is a database hosting platform in the cloud that automatically manages several things, such as recovery on node failure and keeping several nodes in different locations in sync.

To use RDS, go to the services tab and click on Relational Database Service. To create your database, click on **Get Started**, which will take you though a simple setup process.

Once your database has been configured and created, you can use the **endpoint** variable listed on the RDS dashboard and the database name and password to create the SQLAlchemy URL in your production configuration object:

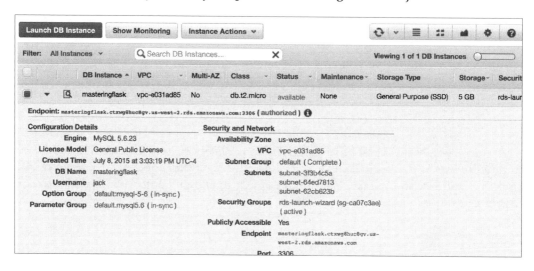

This's all that it takes to create a very resilient database on the cloud with Flask!

Using Celery with Amazon Simple Queue Service

In order to use Celery on AWS, we need to have our Elastic Beanstalk instance run our Celery worker in the background as well as set up **a Simple Queue Service (SQS)** messaging queue. For Celery to support SQS, it needs to install a helper library from `pip`:

```
$ pip install boto
```

Setting up a new messaging queue on SQS is very easy. Go to the services tab and click on **Simple Queue Service** in the applications tab and then click on **Create New Queue.** After a very short configuration screen, you should see a screen much like the following:

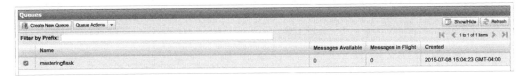

Now we have to change our `CELERY_BROKER_URL` and `CELERY_BACKEND_URL` to the new URL, which takes the following format:

```
sqs://aws_access_key_id:aws_secret_access_key@
```

This uses the key pair you created in the Elastic Beanstalk section.

Finally, we need to tell Elastic Beanstalk to run a Celery worker in the background. We can do this with the `.conf` file in a new directory at the root of the project named `.ebextensions` (note the period at the start of the folder name). In a file in this new directory, it can be called whatever you wish, add the following commands:

```
celery_start:
    command: celery multi start worker1 -A celery_runner
```

Now whenever the instance reboots, this command will be run before the server is run.

Summary

As this chapter explained, there are many different options to hosting your application, each having their own pros and cons. Deciding on one depends on the amount of time and money you are willing to spend as well as the total number of users you expect.

Now we have reached the conclusion of the book. I hope that this book was helpful to build your understanding of Flask and how it can be used to create applications of any complexity with ease and with simple maintainability.

Index

Thank you for buying
Mastering Flask

About Packt Publishing

Packt, pronounced 'packed', published its first book, *Mastering phpMyAdmin for Effective MySQL Management*, in April 2004, and subsequently continued to specialize in publishing highly focused books on specific technologies and solutions.

Our books and publications share the experiences of your fellow IT professionals in adapting and customizing today's systems, applications, and frameworks. Our solution-based books give you the knowledge and power to customize the software and technologies you're using to get the job done. Packt books are more specific and less general than the IT books you have seen in the past. Our unique business model allows us to bring you more focused information, giving you more of what you need to know, and less of what you don't.

Packt is a modern yet unique publishing company that focuses on producing quality, cutting-edge books for communities of developers, administrators, and newbies alike. For more information, please visit our website at www.packtpub.com.

About Packt Open Source

In 2010, Packt launched two new brands, Packt Open Source and Packt Enterprise, in order to continue its focus on specialization. This book is part of the Packt Open Source brand, home to books published on software built around open source licenses, and offering information to anybody from advanced developers to budding web designers. The Open Source brand also runs Packt's Open Source Royalty Scheme, by which Packt gives a royalty to each open source project about whose software a book is sold.

Writing for Packt

We welcome all inquiries from people who are interested in authoring. Book proposals should be sent to author@packtpub.com. If your book idea is still at an early stage and you would like to discuss it first before writing a formal book proposal, then please contact us; one of our commissioning editors will get in touch with you.

We're not just looking for published authors; if you have strong technical skills but no writing experience, our experienced editors can help you develop a writing career, or simply get some additional reward for your expertise.

Rapid Flask

ISBN: 978-1-78355-425-6   Duration: 42 minutes

Get your web applications up and running in no time with Flask

1. Build a web app using Flask from beginning to end—never touch PHP again!

2. Not just "hello, world"—create a fully functional web app that includes web services, HTML forms, and more.

3. Your apps won't look like they came out of the '90s—learn how to integrate basic styles and icons.

4. Go further—get a glimpse of how to utilize Flask's more popular extensions.

Flask Framework Cookbook

ISBN: 978-1-78398-340-7   Paperback: 258 pages

Over 80 hands-on recipes to help you create small-to-large web applications using Flask

1. Get the most out of the powerful Flask framework while remaining flexible with your design choices.

2. Build end-to-end web applications, right from their installation to the post-deployment stages.

3. Packed with recipes containing lots of sample applications to help you understand the intricacies of the code.

Please check **www.PacktPub.com** for information on our titles

Instant Flask Web Development

ISBN: 978-1-78216-962-8   Paperback: 78 pages

Tap into Flask to build a complete application in a style that you control

1. Learn something new in an Instant!
   A short, fast, focused guide delivering immediate results.

2. Build a small but complete web application with Python and Flask.

3. Explore the basics of web page layout using Twitter Bootstrap and jQuery.

4. Get to know how to validate data entry using HTML forms and WTForms.

Web Development with Django Cookbook

ISBN: 978-1-78328-689-8   Paperback: 294 pages

Over 70 practical recipes to create multilingual, responsive, and scalable websites with Django

1. Improve your skills by developing models, forms, views, and templates.

2. Create a rich user experience using Ajax and other JavaScript techniques.

3. A practical guide to writing and using APIs to import or export data.

Please check **www.PacktPub.com** for information on our titles

Made in the USA
San Bernardino, CA
30 April 2017